youth netball
101
drills

age **7** to **11**

Also available from A & C Black

101 Youth Soccer Drills – Age 7–11
2nd edition
Malcolm Cook

101 Youth Soccer Drills – Age 12–16
2nd edition
Malcolm Cook

101 Youth Netball Drills – Age 12–16
Anna and Chris Sheryn

101 Youth Hockey Drills
Stuart Dempster and Dennis Hay

anna and chris sheryn

youth netball

drills

age **7** to **11**

A & C Black • London

Published in 2005 by
A & C Black Publishers Ltd
37 Soho Square
London W1D 3QZ
www.acblack.com

ISBN 0 7136 7194 7

Acknowledgements
Cover illustration by Alex Williamson
Textual illustrations by Q2A Solutions
All photographs courtesy of Getty Images

A & C Black uses paper produced with elemental chlorine-free pulp, harvested from managed sustainable forests.

Typeset in 10/12pt DIN regular
Printed and bound in Great Britain by The Cromwell Press, Trowbridge, Wiltshire

CONTENTS

ACKNOWLEDGEMENTS

Thank you to my enthusiastic guinea-pigs at Ashgate Netball Squad and all the children at Cowling Primary School Netball Club. Also, thank you to all those coaches of netball training sessions I have enjoyed over the years, from school to county.

INTRODUCTION

This book is designed to provide group leaders with a resource to construct effective drills for young netballers. It is intended to provide the basic skills and concepts that will be at the heart of any good player. For this reason you will see the common themes of movement and core passing and catching skills running through many of the drills. It would therefore be very easy for sessions to become repetitive and uninspiring, but it is important to remember that the key objective of any training session with this age group is to ensure that the players want to come back for the next one.

Their experience in these most important of years can determine whether or not they continue to play (at any level) into adult life and will, in many cases, colour their view of sport in general. All players, and in particular younger players, need to have fun – so it's important not to burden them with abstract concepts. If they can learn and not notice that they are doing so, then you have succeeded.

KEY TO DIAGRAMS

GS	Goal Shooter
GA	Goal Attack
WA	Wing Attack
C	Centre
WD	Wing Defence
GD	Goal Defence
GK	Goal Keeper
△	cones
- - - - - - ➤	movement of ball
──────➤	movement of player

SESSION GUIDELINES

communication

In any sport, on most training nights you will see a coach working with young players struggling to form them into pre-drill formations. Instructions such as 'Get into a circle' or 'I need two staggered lines' often result in formations that owe more to a stage farce than a netball session. This leads to exasperated coaches, confused children and wasted time.

Never fear – here are some tips to help overcome some common problems:

Watch your language

I know an excellent tennis coach who, when working with a group of 6–8-year-olds, told them to 'Stand in the tramlines'. I mentioned to him afterwards that the reason that not all of them responded was that many of them had no idea what a tramline was, and even less idea which area of the court he was talking about.

Try at all times to take account of the age and experience of your players before you speak. Avoid jargon like the plague, explain what you mean and constantly question and re-evaluate your use of language. If you want to test yourself, ask a non-netballer to watch a session and keep a list of all the terms that they do not understand. Have a look at the list and then ask yourself what you really meant! For example, if you refer to the 'D', be aware that most seven- or eight-year-olds will know 'the letter D' as 'the duh sound', and in their world a 'D' is actually a 'd' and looks nothing like what you wish to convey.

'Get into pairs/groups of three etc.'

This instruction will rarely elicit a prompt response as junior politics will come into play ('where's my best friend' etc.) and few players will have the foresight to move around to find a partner.

With young players, the best way to deal with this is to designate two points (or markers) as 'Ones' and 'Twos'. Then simply touch each player on the head, look her in the eye (important!) and give her a number. As soon as a player has a number, she should go and stand at the relevant marker. (Top tip: make sure that the markers are well spaced – if they are too close, the groups will intermingle and when you look around you will find that you have only created another heaving mass of humanity elsewhere on the court.) Then the first player in the 'Ones' line pairs up with the first player in the 'Twos' line, and so on.

You can pair up older players by asking everyone to put their hands in the air and keep them there until they have a partner. In this way it is easier for everyone to see who remains.

'Make a circle'

Ask a group of players (of almost any age) to form a circle, and what you get will likely resemble a football crowd. A good way to achieve an evenly spaced circle is to ask all the players to hold hands and then slowly walk backwards as far as they can without letting go. You will be left with an evenly spaced circle.

'Form a staggered line'

In a number of the drills in this book you will need the players to form two parallel lines in a zigzag formation. This, again, can be a real struggle. The easy way to do this is in four steps:

1   Ask the players to form a single line and then hold hands.
2   Spread them out until they can only just hold onto each other – they will then be evenly spaced.
3   Number alternate players one and two – 'One, two, one, two' etc.
4   All number ones stand still. All number twos walk out to form the second line. When both lines turn to face each other, they will form the perfect 'zigzag'.

building drills

When you are introducing complex drills to groups of players, always explain each element separately so that everyone is clear about what they have to do before they start. By flooding the group with information, you run the risk of the drill becoming disorganised or falling apart. For example, if the drill involves a run–receive–land– pass sequence, demonstrate and describe the run and land only at first so that everyone can see and understand what a good job looks like. Only add the next element when the basics are spot on. There is absolutely no point in introducing a ball to a drill if the running and landing principle is not understood.

quality before quantity every time

Building an environment of excellence can be achieved without becoming boring. Just be very clear and concise about the skills you are about to practise and then concentrate on quality of execution at all times. Do not be drawn into lengthy drills that test stamina and reduce quality of play – short, sharp, top-quality drills will ensure that top-quality play is ingrained.

Remember: 'Practice does not make perfect; it makes permanent'. If sloppiness is part of the training regime, it will become ingrained in performances.

the learning curve

The development of a skill during a group practice will not follow a straight line. It is usual for awareness and concentration initially to be high, and for skills to develop at a corresponding rate. However, as the drill progresses concentration levels will fall and therefore so will players' accuracy. If this is allowed to continue unchecked by the coach, competency levels and enjoyment levels will suffer.

To address this issue, coaches must constantly be aware of the pattern of the players' concentration levels and take time to rest their minds and bodies. Stop the drill, re-communicate the objective and the skills involved and then, once the players are rested and ready – both mentally and physically – start again. If necessary, change the drill to something the players are familiar with and can do, then return to the original drill later. In this way the inevitable decline in competency can be arrested and the development curve can be edged upwards.

confidence

When boys encounter problems they are likely to blame the ball, the weather, the passer – anything but themselves. With girls, the first port of call tends to be their own performance. This means that the coach must ensure that confidence is not undermined by progressing drills too quickly for the ability of the players. Instead, provide drills that provide initial success, and progress slowly. Always focus on what has gone right and not on perceived failures.

warming up

A 'warm-up' is necessary to prepare the body for exercise but, contrary to traditional wisdom, there is no evidence that stretching *before* exercise improves performance or reduces the risks of injury. Instead, stretches should be performed *after* exercise.

In comparison, a warm-up should consist of similar movements to the exercises players are about to perform. There is no point running around the court for ten minutes if you are then going to perform a series of sprints or jumps. Think about the range of movements that you are preparing the players for and gradually build up the intensity from gentle warm-up to near-performance level.

Be careful not to warm-up for too long to avoid using up energy that should be reserved for playing. Players will need to sweat a little, but shouldn't be fatigued by the warm-up. A good rule of thumb is to elevate the heart rate to the extent that players are sweating lightly and are mildly out of breath.

warming down

This is a much ignored area of coaching sessions. The last five minutes (at least) of a session should be given over to warming down. This can be done by simply running slowly once around the court followed by two or three stretching drills (see Chapter 8) and a slow jog or walk around the court to finish.

As mentioned above, the warm-down is the place to work on flexibility, and if stretches are carried out consistently players should not experience stiffness in the days following practice or matches. Following exercise the soft tissues will be warm and as a result their inherent ability to stretch will be increased, so any attempts to increase basic flexibility should be carried out in this period. For example, if players have one or two areas that they know are tight (such as the hamstrings or calf muscles), it would be sensible to specifically target these areas with stretches during the warm-down.

drill categories

The drills in this book are divided into the following categories:

1 Warming up
2 Movement and footwork
3 Ball skills – passing and catching
4 Attacking and defending
5 Shooting
6 Game scenarios
7 Warming down

session structure

There are as many ways to compile a session as there are coaches. There are, how-ever, some basic guidelines that will help a session make sense for players and coaches alike. A one-hour session might look like this:

1 Warm-up (10 minutes): while this is taking place, let the players know what the objective is for the session and – most importantly – why this objective is important.
2 Drills (25 minutes): these should be taken from the sections that cover ball skills, movement, attacking and defending, and shooting. Try to focus on one common skill even if you are covering more than one topic so that everyone is clear at the end of the session what has been learned.
3 Game scenarios (15 minutes): these involve plenty of fun and require lots of energy. Only stop the action when the key skills need to be reaffirmed and some order returned.
4 Warm-down and flexibility (10 minutes): Don't skimp on this section. Young players will have less need for flexibility development than adult players but warming down is an invaluable habit to get into. The warm-down is also a great opportunity to reaffirm what has just been practised and reiterate key learning points.

Players of all ages have one thing in common – they prefer playing to practising. With this in mind, make sure that sessions are fun. A sense of humour on court is essential as it not only keeps the coach sane, but also removes the tension that can make players less inclined to extend themselves and risk mistakes.

improvising equipment

There are few groups that enjoy unlimited budgets, so here are some ideas for ways to improvise kit.

Ideally	Alternatives
Beanbags	Rolled-up football socks or socks filled with dried peas and sewn closed
Hoops	Chalk circles or lengths of rope tied into a loop
Cones	Margarine lids and some poster paint to provide colour designations when required.
Skipping ropes	Lengths of washing line make excellent substitutes and in fact are far superior to rope, which turns far too slowly
Bibs	Old T-shirts with the necks and arms cut off, painted with cold-water dyes and spray-painted letters – this might not look good but is great fun for kids to make and saves lots of money

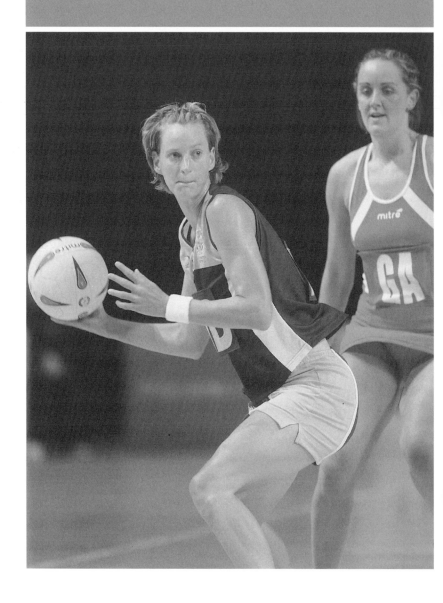

Charlene du Toit (South Africa) looks for her next pass, marked by Tracey Neville (England).

WARMING UP

As previously mentioned, the warm-up is an important part of the session. While there is no evidence to prove that a warm-up aids performance or helps to avoid injuries, experience tells us that a relevant and focused warm-up prepares both mind and body for the practice. The warm-up is also an opportunity for the players to weigh up a new coach, so if you are new to the group make sure that your session is well planned, clear, well delivered and, above all, fun!

Contrary to traditional wisdom, the warm-up is not the place to improve flexibility (save this for the warm-down when the muscles are warm). The warm-up should be controlled and replicate the types of activities that you will be focusing on in the body of the session. So, three times around the court then touch your toes is not really what we are after!

The following drills provide some ideas for warming up with and without the ball. Always follow the same rule – build speed and intensity gradually and focus on quality of movement at all times.

drill 1 *court vocabulary*

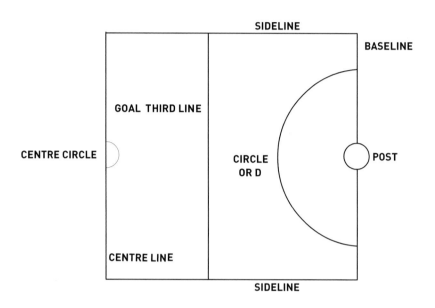

Objective: To warm-up the body and ensure everyone is familiar with the different areas of the court. This drill is ideal for new netballers and youngsters, and not so bad for experienced players either!

Equipment: Half the court.

Description: Spread the players around the area. The coach shouts out the name of one of the lines and points on half a court (e.g. 'side line!') and all the players race to that point. The coach then shouts another position (e.g. 'D!') and the players race there.

Coaching points: When working with new or younger players, add different points slowly, starting by repeating two or three and only adding one at a time. In this way the positions will become ingrained.

Progression: With older players, ask them to move around the half court and then call two or three points in quick succession. The players then have to make a quick decision on the fastest way to reach all points.

drill 2 *froggies*

Objective: To warm up the body and develop explosive power for jumping and speed work.

Equipment: Half the court.

Description: The players start on the side line, squatting with their hands flat on the floor and hands between their knees. On coach's command, each 'frog' must spring as high as possible and land again in the starting position. For fun, the players can compete for the loudest or best 'froggy' sound. Five springs forwards is plenty, then players walk back to the start. Repeat three times.

Coaching points: Concentrate on height and form at all times, ensuring that the players return to the start position before performing the next repetition. As they tire, they will be tempted to jump from a semi-squat position. This will not deliver the same benefit.

drill 3 *creepy crabs*

Objective: To increase the body's range of movement.

Equipment: Half the court.

Description: The players start by standing on the side line facing one end of the court. On the coach's signal, they start moving sideways into the centre of the court. The drill should be performed in both directions, left to right and right to left. Make it fun by asking the players to imitate a crab with nippy pincers (hands) and lots of crabby noises!

Coaching points: It is important that the path of movement is sideways and that the upper body doesn't creep around. To achieve this, the players should perform the drill while the coach remains on the side line. The players must look at the coach as they perform the drill, which will stop them from twisting.

drill 4 *jumping crabs*

Objective: To increase the body's range of movement.

Equipment: Half the court.

Description: The players start by standing on the side line facing one end of the court. On the coach's signal, they start jumping sideways into the centre of the court. The drill should be performed in both directions, left to right and right to left.

Coaching points: It is important that the path of movement is sideways and that the upper body doesn't creep around. To achieve this, the players should perform the drill while the coach remains on the side line. The players must look at the coach as they perform the drill, which will stop them from twisting.

The objective of this drill is to achieve height and 'hang-time', so encourage the use of arms to drive the body up and gain height.

drill 5 *fast mice*

Objective: To warm up the body and develop foot speed.

Equipment: Half the court.

Description: The players start by standing on the side line facing into court. They then have to reach the centre of the court using very fast feet and tiny steps. The objective is to complete as many tiny steps in the shortest amount of time. As with all these animal drills, you can make it as fun as possible by asking the players to imitate a mouse – noises and all.

Coaching points: Younger children will lose concentration and form very quickly and will increase the step length in order to move forwards quickly. Re-emphasise the objective of the drill before each re-start. The race is not to see who moves forwards fastest, but who can get the most steps in during the specified distance. Ensure that the forward motion is steady.

Progression: Try a timed race – who can perform the most steps in, for example, 10 seconds.

drill 6 *stomping giants*

Objective: To develop strength and improve movement abilities.

Equipment: Half the court.

Description: More foolishness! Starting on the side line, ask the players to march out to the centre of the court pretending to be the biggest, loudest giant imaginable. Each stride must be as long as possible, each leg lift must be as high as possible and the drill must be performed under control. The objective is perfect form, not speed.

Coaching points: Encourage straight legs during this drill.

Progression: Give each 'giant' a marker (anything will do – margarine-tub lids are fine). Ask players to stomp out for eight strides, put down the marker and, after walking back to the start, try to reach their marker in fewer strides the next time.

Objective: To encourage concentration using a fun warm-up.

Equipment: Players.

Description: On the coach's command the players must form groups as per the instruction. For example, if the coach calls 'Fours!' the players must form groups of four, all holding hands with each other, and so on.

Coaching points: Once the players have grasped the principle of this drill it can be introduced unexpectedly (with a prize for the first group to form correctly – chocolate buttons work wonders!) into any part of the session, just to keep everyone on their toes.

Progression: Add four different coloured cones around the perimeter of the working area. On the coach's command all the players have to run around the designated cone before forming into their groups.

drill 8 *dodge tag*

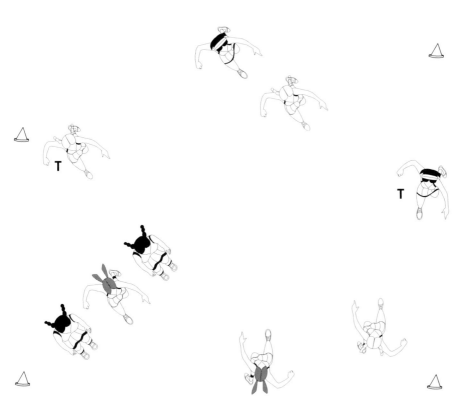

Objective: To practise dodging skills and improve balanced movement.

Equipment: Players.

Description: The playing area selected should be sufficient to allow the players to run around but not so large that it allows full freedom of movement. One third of the court is ideal, or you can reduce the size of the area of movement using cones. Two players are taggers (T). The rest of the players must dodge out of their way and avoid being tagged. Players who have been tagged must stand still, creating barriers for the other players to dodge around.

Coaching points: Youngsters can get a bit excited and run into each other. Watch out for controlled movement and encourage players to avoid each other. One danger is players being hit by flailing arms, so warn the group first.

Progression: Reduce the size of the playing area and increase the number of players 'on'.

drill 9 *snakes*

Objective: To warm up and have fun!

Equipment: One ball per team.

Description: Divide the group into teams, with a maximum of six players per team. Each team lines up with the players one behind the other, 1 m apart with legs apart. Player A is the first player in the line and has the ball. On the coach's command, A rolls the ball through the legs of the other players in her line, then races to take up position at the end of the line and catch her own roll. Facing forwards, she picks up the ball and passes it to the player in front, who takes the ball in both hands and twists the opposite way to give the ball to the next player. This left/right twisting motion is repeated until the ball is with the player at the front of the line, who starts the drill again by rolling the ball through the tunnel of legs once more. Repeat until all players have rolled.

Coaching points: While this is a 'young' drill, the twisting motion is a great warm-up for the upper body and with two teams racing each other it can be a lot of fun.

drill 10 *name game*

Objective: To warm up the body and have fun.

Equipment: Cones.

Description: Use the cones to set up a five-metre long grid. The players line up at the start line. The coach calls out a series of instructions; if an instruction applies to a player or players, they must run to the opposite side of the grid and back again. For example, 'All players with blonde hair; whose name begins with S'; who have a brother' and so on.

Coaching points: Look for short steps as the players accelerate, driving back with their elbows to pump the arms. The turn at the opposite side of the grid should be a sharp change of direction, not a slow curve. The players should drive away from this line too.

drill 11 *duck duck goose*

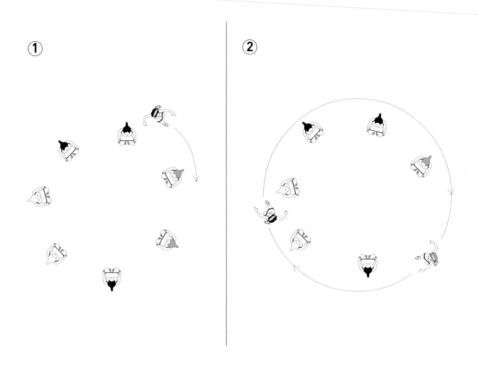

Objective: To develop balance when running, speed and quick reactions.

Equipment: Players.

Description: Choose one player to be the 'goose'; all other players are 'ducks'. The ducks sit in a circle facing inwards, with the goose on the outside of the circle. The goose walks around the circle behind the ducks, saying 'duck, duck, duck ...' as she passes each one. At random, the goose shouts 'goose' and taps the head of the duck she is standing behind. The aim is for the goose to run around the circle and take the space left by the duck before the duck catches her. The duck who is tapped on the head has to get up and chase the goose around the circle, aiming to tag the goose before she reaches the space in the circle.

Coaching points: Encourage runners to run close to the circle, using both arms and legs to help them run quickly and in control.

drill 12 *ladders*

Objective: To develop balance while running, speed and quick reactions.

Equipment: Players.

Description: Pair players of similar ability and arrange as shown above, sitting facing each other with legs stretched out to make the rungs of a ladder. There should be a one-arm gap between the players in each team. Number the pairs 1, 2, 3 etc. The coach shouts a number and that pair have to jump up and race up and down the ladder. The drill is a race between the two teams to see who can get back to the starting place first.

Coaching points: It is important that the players keep their legs flat throughout the game to avoid tripping up the runners. The players also need to keep their hands close to their own bottom, or fingers will be stepped on.

Progression: More than one number can be called at once.

drill 13 *catch!*

Objective: To develop hand–eye co-ordination and confident catching.

Equipment: A bucket of tennis balls (or sponge balls for younger children) and one racket.

Description: The players space out in a large playing area. The coach stands facing them and hits the balls high into the air with the racket. This should be done as quickly as possible. The children have to catch the tennis balls and return them to the bucket. If there are lots of players, it may be safer to have a separate bucket to replace the balls to avoid players running into the coach or tennis racket!

Coaching points: Keep the balls flying thick and fast and vary the direction. Encourage the players to move their feet to get under the ball to catch it and keep their eye on the ball – they should watch it into their hands.

Progression: This can be played in teams with one hoop per team to collect retrieved balls. The winning team retrieves the most balls.

drill 14 ball thief

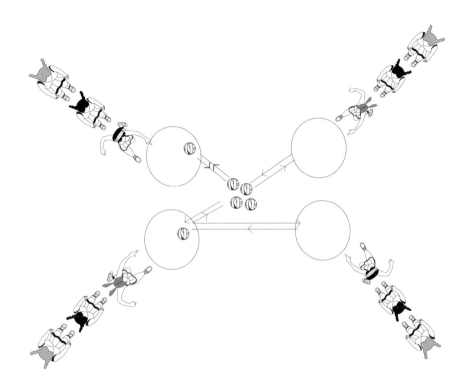

Objective: To warm up and develop good communication and speed.

Equipment: Four hoops and six balls.

Description: Place one hoop at each corner of a 5 m square. The hoops are 'home base' for each team. Divide the players into four teams and stand them in line, one team behind each base. Place eight balls in the centre of the square. On the coach's command, one player from each team runs to the centre to grab one (and only one) ball, before returning to place the ball in their hoop. Then the next player in line runs to grab another ball. Once all the balls have gone from the centre the runners can steal a ball from the other bases. This continues until one team has three balls in their hoop. If no-one wins in a set time the coach can add another ball or two to make success a little easier.

Coaching points: Watch out for cheats picking up two balls at a time or stealing from bases before all the central balls have gone! Also watch for more than one player per team running at once. Encourage each team to talk to their runner so she knows what is going on around her.

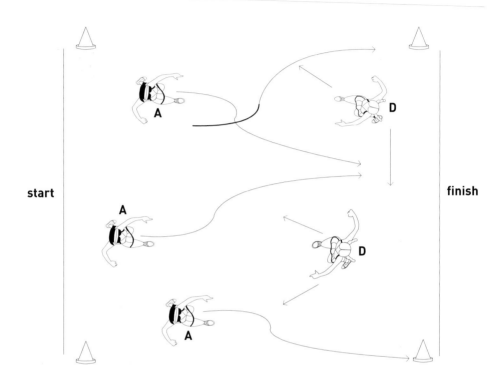

start   finish

Objective: To warm up by running, dodging and reacting to other players.

Equipment: Four cones.

Description: The size of the area used should reflect the age and number of players. Two or three defenders (D) stand in the middle of the playing area. On the coach's whistle the other players (attackers or A) try to cross 'the wall' of defenders to reach the other side of the playing area without being tagged. If a player is tagged she joins the defending wall.

Coaching points: Keep the grid small to encourage dodging and sprinting. Ensure players tag below shoulder height for safety.

Progression: Change the footwork patterns of the defending wall and running players. For example, they can run using side steps, and dodge using a push off one foot to change direction.

drill 16 *reaction drill*

Objective: To practise quick reactions and to develop hand–eye co-ordination.

Equipment: One ball between two players.

Description: Player A is working, with player B feeding the ball. Player A stands opposite player B, approximately 1 m apart. Player A lightly places her hands on her head. Player B drops the ball from different heights in front of player A, who tries to catch the ball before it hits the ground. The players take it in turns to catch the ball.

Coaching points: Quick reaction time is the key so players need to concentrate.

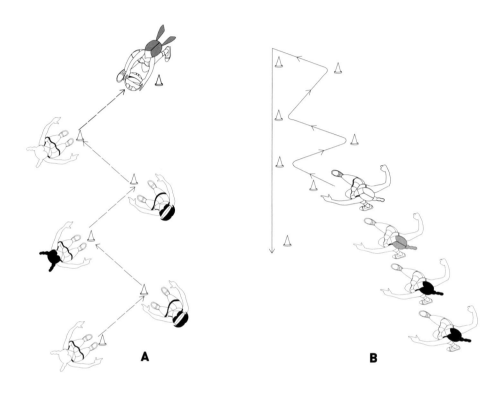

A   **B**

Objective: To warm up and practise passing skills. This drill may be unsuitable for younger players.

Equipment: One ball, cones.

Description: Divide the players into two teams. One team (A) spreads out in a zigzag formation about 3 m apart using half a court. This team passes the ball continuously up and down the zigzag. At the same time, the other team (B) runs in a zigzag over approximately two thirds of a court, running one at a time in relay fashion. The passing team counts the number of passes completed in the time it takes all the runners to complete the course. Any pass dropped is not to be added to the total. The teams then reverse roles and compare scores.

Coaching points: Look for accurate, balanced passing. For the runners, movement should be balanced and controlled using quick steps.

Progression: Vary the type of pass used. Vary the footwork pattern used.

drill 18 *horse and jockey*

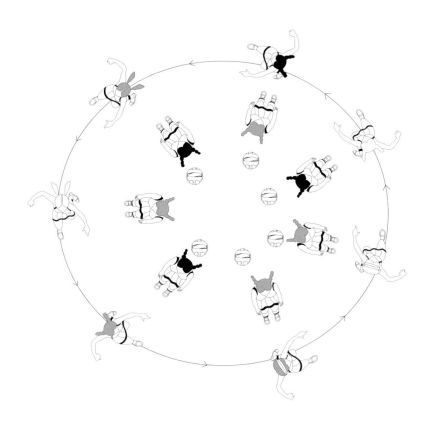

Objective: To warm up the body.

Equipment: Several balls.

Description: Split the players into two teams of equal numbers and arrange them in two circles, one inside the other. A number of balls are placed in the middle of the inner circle. On the call of 'left' or 'right' the players in the outside circle have to run in that direction around the entire circle. Once the players get back to their starting positions they must go through the legs of a player in the inner circle and grab a ball. Players need to be on their feet before going for a ball.

Coaching points: Ensure plenty of rest between goes. This will ensure that the players practise high-quality speed and agility over a short distance.

Progression: The number of balls can be varied. For example, to increase the competition you can reduce the number of balls so only the quickest players get a ball.

drill 19 copycats

Objective: To improve reactions and get players moving.

Equipment: One third of the court and one ball.

Description: The players space out in one third of the court and stand facing the coach, who stands in the centre circle with a ball. On command, all players start 'fast feet' on the spot and watch the ball. The coach moves the ball to different positions at random, for example high left, high right, in front and so on. All the players must react by stretching their arms in the same direction as the ball.

Coaching points: Look for players maintaining fast feet throughout – the movement should be balanced and controlled. Encourage quick reactions.

Progression: The coach throws the ball up, left or right, and players react by jumping in the relevant direction. The coach drops the ball, and players react by touching the floor (straight down, to the left, or to the right) and immediately jumping back up. The coach can also drop the ball behind her, at which point all players must sprint to the opposite goal third. (For young players, keep sprints to a minimum.)

drill 20 *run rabbit*

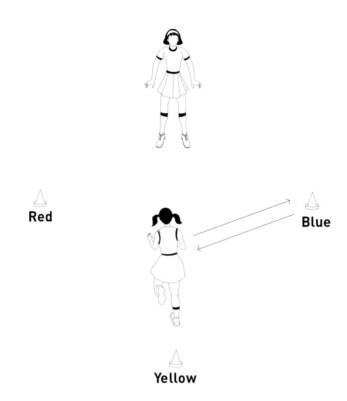

Red

Blue

Yellow

Objective: To improve reactions and get players moving.

Equipment: Three different coloured cones between two players.

Description: Set out the cones in a triangle with approximately 2 m between each cone. Player 1 is working and starts in the centre of the triangle. Player 2 stands outside the triangle facing player 1. Player 1 starts fast feet movements on the spot. Player 2 will shout a colour to player 1, who must react by quickly moving to the correct coloured cone, touching it and returning to the centre of the triangle, facing player 2 at all times. When player 1 has returned to the centre, player 2 shouts out another colour. After a short time, swap roles.

Coaching points: Look for players maintaining fast feet throughout. The movement should be balanced and controlled. The working player should use side steps, quick steps backwards and so on to reach each cone. Encourage quick reactions and watch for players staying facing each other throughout.

Progression: Add another cone. Increase the working area.

drill 21 *hopscotch passing*

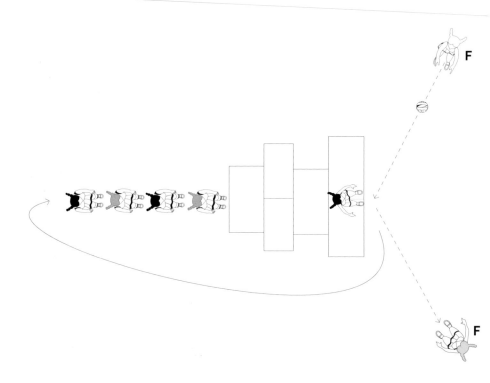

Objective: To warm up, introducing the ball and throwing and catching.

Equipment: One ball and chalk.

Description: Chalk out a hopscotch grid. Two feeders (F) stand about 3 m from the end of the grid, 3 m apart. One of the feeders has the ball. On the coach's command, the first player hop-scotches down the grid. When she lands (two footed) at the end, she receives a chest pass from the feeder and passes to the other feeder. The player then runs straight back, high-fives the next player and goes to the back of the queue.

Coaching points: Encourage fast feet throughout the hopscotch grid. Ensure that the players hit every step or hop accurately and treat the squares as if they are red hot. With younger players speed should be built up slowly and never sought at the expense of accuracy. Look for quick, accurate passing.

Progression: Vary the type of pass. Increase the distance between feeders and the end of the grid. Set up a straight race between two groups. As the players gain confidence, introduce a pivot between receiving and giving the pass.

MOVEMENT AND FOOTWORK

Movement in netball is all about agility, change of speed and direction, control and balance. The footwork rule is a basic skill for young players to learn; once players are more confident with the idea of controlling momentum and are able to apply the footwork rule in the majority of situations, coaching can move on to focus on improving balance and control.

Landing is an important skill to master. Jumping to catch the ball can help to control forward momentum and enable you to land without stepping. If you jump up to catch the ball it is much safer to land on both feet. However, learning to land on one foot and then pivot helps to change the direction of the game, allowing players to use open spaces and move the ball into different areas of the court. Pivoting is another key skill for young players to get to grips with. Eventually, landing on one foot leads to the running pass for more experienced players. Here the ball is released quickly while the player is still on the move, speeding up the game and creating attacking opportunities.

When working with younger players, coaches must remember that halting a moving body requires a considerable amount of strength. Keep drills involving lots of changes of direction nice and brief so that quality remains high. There is no harm in rest!

In this chapter, the basic footwork rule has been broken down into simple component parts to help young, inexperienced players understand fully what is involved. Coaches may select the level of drill they want to use depending on the experience and ability of the players. The emphasis is still on having fun and the drills are designed to reinforce the skills needed in key areas through repetition in different situations. The coach must focus on quality throughout.

drill 22 cat and mouse

Objective: To develop spatial awareness and improve movement skills.

Equipment: One beanbag or football sock between two players.

Description: Divide the group into pairs. One is a mouse and the other a cat. The mouse tucks a 'tail' (the beanbag or sock) into the back of her waistband. The cat must see how quickly she can grab the tail. This drill is designed to help dodging skills so it is a good idea to remove the possibility of the mouse simply running off by restricting the space available, for example to one third of the court only.

Coaching points: Try to ensure that there is plenty of face-to-face dodging instead of just running and chasing.

Progression: To add some more fun have two cats and lots of mice in the playing area. If a mouse tail is grabbed, that mouse must replace her tail and wait, with legs wide, until a live mouse crawls through her legs to bring her back to life. Keep changing the cats and see how many tails they can catch in two minutes.

drill 23 *follow the leader*

Objective: To practise the different footwork steps used in netball.

Equipment: The whole court.

Description: Select a leader (the coach may need to be leader to show the players the correct footwork patterns to use). Starting at one corner of the base line, the other players follow the leader using the same steps and footwork patterns. Follow the directions as shown above, or let the leader choose the direction. The coach should choose from jogging, sprinting, side steps, and backward steps.

Coaching points: The aim is to keep the weight balanced, moving forwards with quick changes of direction pushing off from the outside foot.

Progression: For older players, introduce cross-over steps around the circle edge. This involves a sideways movement with one foot crossing over the front of the other. The weight should be slightly forwards on the front of the foot. Players need to use hips and shoulders to keep the movement balanced.

drill 24 *cats and dogs*

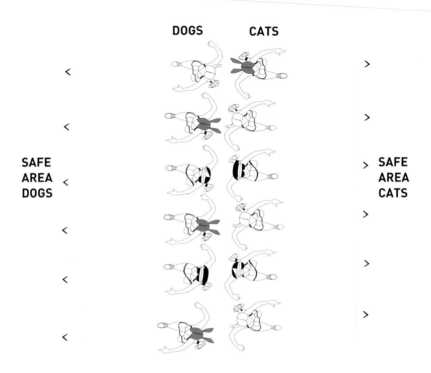

DOGS **CATS**

**SAFE
AREA
DOGS**

**SAFE
AREA
CATS**

Objective: To practise quick movement and improve reactions.

Equipment: Cones.

Description: Line the players up in two lines back to back. Start with either everyone standing or everyone sitting. One line is called the 'Cats' and the other line the 'Dogs'. If 'Cats' is called out by the coach, the players in that line have to run to a designated area, chased by their 'Dog' partner. If 'Dog' is called out, the 'Dogs' run and the 'Cats' chase.

Coaching points: Look for balanced movement, and quick responses.

Progression: Increase the working area to encourage more sprinting or decrease it to encourage more dodging.

drill 25 *small compass game*

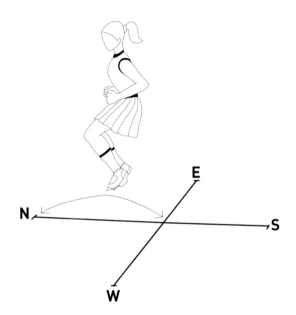

Objective: To improve reactions and develop speed of jumps.

Equipment: Chalk and pairs of players.

Description: Chalk a compass on the floor for each pair (from the centre to each compass point should be 50–75 cm – you may need to experiment to gauge the ability of the group). Player one starts with both feet on the centre of the compass in a ready position. The coach calls out a compass point and the player jumps to that point and back again as quickly as possible. The jump is with feet together, facing the coach at all times. North will be a forward then backward jump, South backward then forward and so on. Once the players have got the hang of it, call out a series of points in quick succession and use this as a reaction drill. Work each player for no more than 30 seconds at a time before swapping them over.

Coaching points: There will be a tendency for players' feet to come apart so that the jump becomes a step. If younger players struggle with the points of a compass, swap them for coloured chalk points or numbers.

Objective: To develop reactions, speed and control of landings.

Equipment: Chalk.

Description: Divide the players into pairs. Chalk a star on the floor for each pair; from the centre of the star to each point should measure between 75 cm and 1 m (you may have to experiment while you gauge the ability of the group). Number the points 1–5. Player one is working while player two is resting. Player one starts with both feet together at the centre of the star in a ready position. The coach calls out a point (for example, 'One!') and the player jumps to that point as quickly as possible. The jump is with one foot, ending with a solid two-footed landing. Players should face the coach at all times so will have to jump backwards or sideways to some of the points. Work each player for no more than 30 seconds at a time before swapping pairs over and watch for quality at all times.

Coaching points: Focus on the landing and do not rush the return to the start position, or the learning point will be lost.

drill 27 ball tag

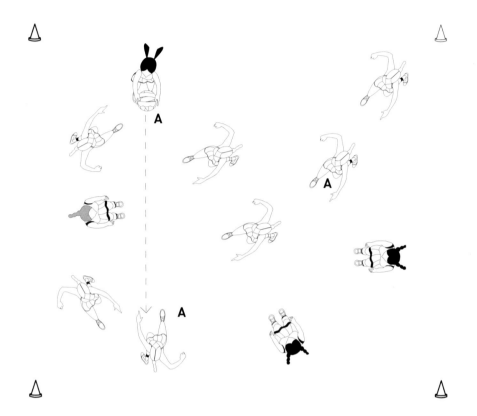

Objective: To practise quick passing and dodging, and to develop teamwork.

Equipment: One ball and four cones.

Description: You need three attackers and at least five evaders. Mark out a section of court with the cones (a 5 m square will do for these numbers). The attackers have the ball and their aim is to tag an evader with the ball. Once tagged, the evaders must stand still. The attackers cannot run when in possession of the ball, but can pivot on one foot. The attackers must work to trap the evaders and then call for the pass.

Coaching points: Tagging is done by touching (not throwing) the ball onto the evader. Players may tend to stand still and wait for the pass, so encourage them to work together to achieve the objective. Keep the evader teams small to avoid a lot of waiting around; with a big group, increase the number of attackers and the size of the grid. Encourage communication and movement between the attackers, looking for quick, accurate passing.

Progression: See how many evaders the attackers can tag in a certain time.

drill 28 *the pivot 1*

Objective: To introduce pivoting.

Equipment: Two hoops, five beanbags, chalk.

Description: Place the hoops about 1 m apart and chalk a cross on the ground exactly in between. Put the beanbags in the hoop on the left. The player starts by standing with her left foot on the cross. On the coach's command, she pivots towards the hoop with the beanbags in it, keeping her left foot on the cross at all times. She reaches down and picks up one beanbag, then pivots on her left foot again to drop the beanbag in the opposite hoop. Repeat until all the beanbags have been moved.

Coaching points: Encourage the players to get the feel of the pivoting movement on one foot. The stationary foot (which would be the landing foot in a game) must stay on the cross throughout the drill. The players need to be on their toes and should not drag the landing foot to move off the cross.

Progression: Once everyone has completed the drill pivoting on the left foot, repeat with the right foot on the cross and the beanbags being passed right to left.

drill 29 the pivot 2

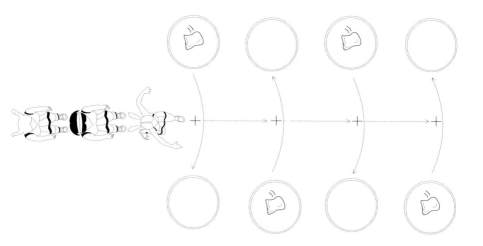

Objective: To progress the pivoting learning process.

Equipment: Eight hoops, four beanbags and chalk.

Description: Place the hoops in two lines of four approximately 1 m apart with a chalked cross in between each pair of hoops. Put one beanbag in diagonally opposite hoops, as shown above. The first player walks into the grid, places her right foot on the cross and pivots to pick up the bean bag on the right and then places the bag in the hoop on the left. The player then progresses up the grid pivoting alternately left and right to pick up and put down the bags in the hoop. On completion player two enters the grid and repeats the drill (obviously player two will start on the opposite side).

Coaching points: Encourage the players to get the feel of the pivoting movement and keep the landing foot still throughout the drill.

Progression: Set up two grids and two groups and race to see who can complete the drill first.

drill 30 *the pivot 3*

Objective: To progress the pivoting learning process. This drill may have to be reserved for more experienced players.

Equipment: Eight cones, one ball, chalk.

Description: Set the cones out in a staggered grid with a feeder on each cone and chalked crosses between each pair of cones (see diagram). The first player walks into the grid, places her right foot on the first cross and pivots to receive a pass from feeder 1 on her right, then pivots to make a pass to feeder 2 on her left. The player progresses up the grid, pivoting alternately left and right to give and receive passes. Player 2 then enters the grid and repeats the drill.

Coaching points: Encourage the players to get the feel of the pivoting movement and keep the landing foot still. Look for players facing the feeders to receive and pass the ball.

Progression: As players become more confident, increase the speed of the drill. Perform the drill as a relay race between two teams.

drill 31 *the stepping rule*

Objective: To introduce the footwork (stepping) rule.

Equipment: Four cones.

Description: Use the cones to mark out a playing area measuring 10 m by 5 m. The players move around freely and, on the coach's whistle, jump, swinging their arms high above their heads to help gain height, and then land one foot after the other. Players then stand still and wait for the instruction to restart.

Coaching points: Young players may find it helpful to count out loud the landing, 'one, two', with 'one' being their landing foot. The jump allows the players to control their forward momentum and therefore land under control without 'stepping'. Ask players which is their landing foot (number one). This is the foot that must stay still to pivot when playing.

Progression: With more experienced players, introduce an alternate left- and right-footed landing. Progress to running and jumping before the landing.

Objective: To introduce the ball once players have mastered the idea of a controlled landing.

Equipment: One ball.

Description: It is best to start with the coach feeding the ball to ensure good quality feeding. Line the players up approximately 5 m from the coach. Player 1 runs towards the coach, jumps, lands and receives a pass. The ball is returned to the coach and player 1 runs to the back of the queue. The second player then repeats the drill.

Coaching points: Try to keep the queues short so that players are not standing around doing nothing. You may need to enlist an extra pair of adult hands to achieve this. Encourage a controlled landing before the ball is passed back to the feeder.

Progression: Gradually increase the distance between the players and the coach.

drill 33 *snakes and ladders*

Objective: To reinforce good footwork.

Equipment: Eight cones.

Description: Use the cones to set up a ladder grid as above with the 'rungs' getting progressively further apart, starting at 1 m and ending at 5 m. All players stand on the start line. On the coach's command, they jog to the first cone, jump and land using good footwork. The players wait for the next command to jog to the second cone, and so on.

Coaching points: Allow a decent break (at least a couple of minutes) between runs to ensure that the players have the feeling of control before they start again. With young players, you can even turn this into a type of musical statues – they jump, land and freeze until the next command.

Progression: Once good practice is ingrained, speed up the run between cones. The faster the run, the more momentum there is to be controlled and therefore the harder the drill. If quality suffers, reduce the speed and build up again.

drill 34 *change direction*

Objective: To practise quick, controlled changes of direction.

Equipment: Half the court.

Description: The players should space out within the working area. On the coach's whistle they jog in a straight line until they meet either a line or another player. When this happens they must change direction quickly by pushing off one foot and turning their body from the hips and shoulders, using their arms to help. Once they are facing in another direction, they carry on jogging until they meet another obstacle.

Coaching points: The change of direction should be a definite move, quick and controlled. The player is aiming to change direction without losing momentum and speed. It helps to exaggerate the arm and body movement, a bit like a child imitating a steam train!

Progression: Once players are comfortable with jogging, try increasing the pace. Cones placed at random in the working area can be added as extra obstacles.

drill 35 *the dodge 1*

Objective: To introduce a dodging movement to young players.

Equipment: Two cones between two players.

Description: Place the cones approximately 3 m apart. The attacker stands in between the cones, with the defender in front of the attacker, facing the same way. The attacker must use side steps along the line between the two cones, pushing off on the outside or leading foot at each cone to change direction. When the attacker side-steps behind the defender for the third time, she must make a dodge movement to change direction quickly. The dodge involves a quick transfer of weight from one side to the other to change direction, pushing off on one foot and using the shoulders to 'turn' the body quickly.

Coaching points: This is not a defending drill so the defender is only acting as a 'prop' for the attacker. The dodge should be a quick, controlled movement.

drill 36 *the dodge 2*

Objective: To practise dodging to receive a pass.

Equipment: One ball and two cones between three players.

Description: Place the cones approximately 3 m apart. The attacker stands in between the cones with the defender in front of the attacker, facing the same way. The feeder stands approximately 3 m away with the ball. The attacker must use side steps along the line between the two cones, pushing off on the outside or leading foot at each cone to change direction. When the whistle blows, the attacker must push off on the leading foot to dodge and receive a chest pass from the feeder.

Coaching points: This is not a defending drill, so initially the defender should stand still. The dodge should be a quick, controlled movement. Look for the attacker pointing to where she wants to receive the ball. The pass should be accurate and quick once the feeder sees the attacker has made her move.

Progression: Allow the defender to move and try to intercept the pass. Move the feeder further away as the players gain confidence.

drill 37 *racing snake*

Objective: To improve speed and agility and practise dodging.

Equipment: Players.

Description: The players line up one behind the other all facing the same way, 2 m apart. On the coach's command, the player at the back of the queue runs up the line, weaving in and out of the standing players and facing the coach (who is standing at the head of the line) at all times. When the player reaches the front, she takes up position at the head of the queue and the next player runs.

Coaching points: Make sure that the runners are facing the front at all times, not following their nose in a looping path. In this way the players will be pushing off the outside foot to change direction. Encourage players to keep their heads up and look forwards rather than looking at their feet.

Progression: As the group improves, decrease the gap between players – the narrower the gap, the harder the player has to work. To introduce an element of competition, form two lines and have a race.

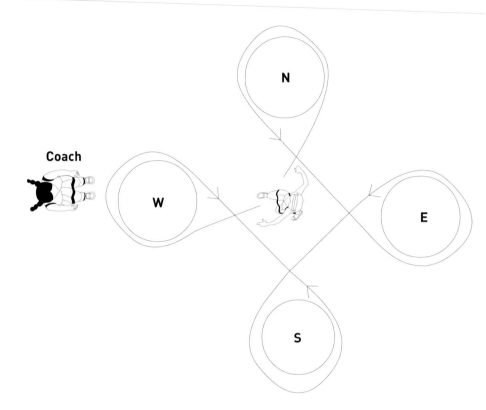

Objective: To develop confidence with different footwork patterns.

Equipment: Four hoops designated North, South, East and West.

Description: Lay out the hoops in a compass formation 3 m apart. Player 1 stands in the centre of the compass and on the coach's command (e.g. 'West') runs around that hoop, facing the coach at all times. The player moves clockwise around the 'compass' until all hoops have been rounded, and then returns home to the centre.

Coaching points: Make sure players face the coach at all times and don't just follow their noses around the hoops. They will have to move sideways and backwards as well as forwards. Encourage players to keep their heads up and look forwards rather than looking at their feet.

Progression: This can be made even more fun by adapting it to 'wink murder' – when the coach winks the players must react by running out to a beanbag or ball outside the 'compass', passing it under each leg, around their back and then finishing with it held on top of their head.

drill 39 the running square

Objective: To introduce the difference between jogging and sprinting.

Equipment: Three cones.

Description: Use the cones to mark out three 3 m sets. You will have the start line and then three further cones. The players line up along the start line and jog to the first cone, accelerate gently to the next cone and sprint at full pace to the final cone. Walk back to the start slowly to recover.

Coaching points: Look for a definite change of pace between the jog and the sprint. Encourage players to use their arms to help increase speed. Players need to be reasonably fresh, so allow plenty of rest between sets to ensure that every set is top quality.

drill 40 *turn and catch*

Objective: To develop quick reactions and catching skills and introduce the idea of turning the body to receive a pass.

Equipment: One ball between two players.

Description: Set up the players approximately 2m apart. Player 2 starts with the ball. Player 1 is working and stands with her back to player 2. Player 2 shouts 'left' or 'right' and player 1 must turn quickly in that direction to receive a pass. Player 2 should only pass the ball once player 1 has turned and is facing her. After five goes, swap roles.

Coaching points: Look for a quick reaction and a controlled turn by player 1. Passes should be accurate.

Progression: Vary the type of pass. Increase the distance between players. When players are turning and receiving the ball confidently, the feeder can pass the ball into the space for the other player to move onto.

drill 41 _footwork relays_

HOP, SKIP, SIDESKIP ETC.

Objective: To develop confidence in different footwork patterns and improve control and balance.

Equipment: Four cones.

Description: Divide the players into two teams. Set up the players in 2 lines as shown. On the coach's whistle, the first player from each team completes the course to the opposite line and tags her team mate, who continues back to her team mate on the opposite line. This continues until all players have completed the course. The coach should shout out different footwork patterns, such as 'jog', 'sprint', 'side step', 'backwards' and so on, and the players have to use these to complete the course.

Coaching points: Look for balanced and controlled footwork. Watch out for cheating!

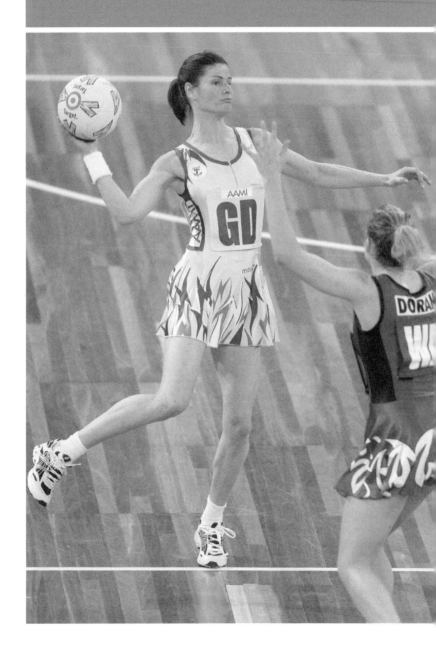

Kathryn Harby Williams (Thunderbirds, Australia) looks to pass the ball using good shoulder-pass technique.

BALL SKILLS – PASSING AND CATCHING

Good ball skills are obviously at the heart of netball, with the game depending on the players' ability to pass the ball with speed and accuracy down the court. Good netballers are able to vary their choice of pass to suit the situation and confidently pass the ball when under pressure from the opposing team's defence.

Good netballers need strong hands for catching and throwing. This is something most young players will lack, so ball skills will need to be developed gradually to improve confidence in throwing and catching and increase strength.

A common issue with younger, inexperienced players is that they consider possession of the ball to be the end in itself rather than a link in a team chain. This results in players following the ball around the court rather than moving into a space to receive it. Coaches need to encourage young players to be aware of the space on court as well as the ball – to think of more than just the next pass, but the next two or three passes.

As skills develop and drills require more movement, balance will become more and more important. Therefore, good practice is vital even within the more simple drills. Encourage a system of check–receive–pass–move, maintaining control and balance at all times.

When passing the ball, tell players that:

- fingers should be well spread to help control the ball
- the weight of the player should be transferred from the back foot to the front foot to help propel the ball and give power to the pass
- the ball should be passed into the space ahead of the catcher's fingers, not behind them!

When catching the ball, tell players that:

- the catcher should watch the ball until it is in their hands
- fingers should be opened wide to receive the ball, with thumbs behind
- the catcher should drive their hands out towards the ball and snatch it back in close to the body.

drill 42 *the clapping game*

Objective: To improve reactions, increase ball awareness and develop passing.

Equipment: One ball.

Description: The players stand in a circle facing inwards. The coach stands in the middle with the ball and chest passes the ball at random to the players in the circle. The players must clap once before they catch the ball and then return the ball to the coach using a chest pass. Players must sit down if they drop the ball, don't clap before they catch the ball or clap to a faked pass.

Coaching points: Ensure quality at all times and do not allow wayward passes. When the players are more confident, they can be the feeders, but it is important that the feeders are able to throw consistent passes to keep the game moving. Players sitting out can join back in after a specified time, for example after three successful consecutive passes, or play until one player is left standing.

Progression: Use two feeders and two balls. Vary the type of pass, and add the rule that players must sit down if they use a different pass from the one in play.

drill 43 *reaction drill*

Objective: To encourage good reactions to the ball.

Equipment: One ball between two players.

Description: The two players face each other approximately 2 m apart. The defender runs on the spot, using quick small steps. The attacker passes or drops the ball in any direction within arm's reach of the defender, who catches and returns the ball to the attacker using a chest pass.

Coaching points: All passes should be quick and are intended to catch the defender off guard. The defender should aim to stay balanced and in control of her movement and passes. Ensure quality at all times and do not allow wayward passes.

Progression: Forfeits can be included for wayward passes from either person or if the defender stops running, for example 10 star jumps.

drill 44 *bounce pass 1*

Objective: To develop confidence and co-ordination.

Equipment: One ball per player.

Description: On the coach's command, each player throws their ball straight up, allows it to bounce and catches it on the way up.

Coaching points: The bounce pass is a low pass used over a short distance, usually to feed the ball into the circle. This drill is the first element for teaching players how to receive a bounce pass.

Progression: Once the players have got the hang of this drill, introduce competition by seeing who can complete three successful repetitions first.

Objective: To develop the bounce pass.

Equipment: One ball per player and a wall.

Description: Each player stands approximately 1 m from the wall and performs a bounce pass against the wall, catching the rebound. The ball should be 'pushed' towards the wall with the fingers pointing downwards.

Coaching points: To help younger players, chalk a cross approximately 30 cm from the wall as a target for the bounce. Ideally, players should not move their feet. In this way, accurate passing will be encouraged.

Progression: As confidence and competence grow try moving the players further from the wall and introduce races, such as the first to five consecutive successful passes.

Objective: To practise the bounce pass.

Equipment: One ball per team.

Description: Divide the group into teams of eight. Set up the teams in a zigzag formation, with approximately 2 m between teams. On the coach's command, the ball is passed up the line using a bounce pass.

Coaching points: Younger players will get excited as they become engrossed in the drill and will want to unload the ball quickly instead of executing a good pass. If this becomes a problem, tell the players that they are responsible for the ball until the receiver has caught it, so if a pass is dropped or missed then the passer has to retrieve it and run back to make a new pass.

Progression: This drill can be made continuous by asking the players to run to the end of the line after they have passed. If you have two teams, an element of competition can be introduced by setting a distance to be covered by the team.

drill 47 *chest pass 1*

Objective: To develop confidence and co-ordination.

Equipment: A wall.

Description: The players stand a stride away from the wall and, keeping the feet still, lean forwards to put both hands flat on the wall with the fingers spread. On the coach's command, the players push away, trying to push themselves back to a standing position.

Coaching points: This is the first element for teaching a chest pass; it is not a strength exercise and should not be treated as such. This drill will give the player the feeling of the passing movement without the complication of having to direct a ball. This drill should be used sparingly as it is not very exciting, but it is a vital learning component when used in conjunction with the next three drills.

Objective: To develop the chest pass.

Equipment: One ball per player and a wall.

Description: The players stand 2 m from the wall and perform a chest pass against the wall, catching the ball on the rebound.

Coaching points: To help younger players, chalk a cross just above head height on the wall as a target for the pass. This will help the players to focus on a target and also begin to appreciate the need to elevate a pass slightly.

Progression: As confidence and competence grow, try moving the players further from the wall and introduce races, for example to see who is the first to five consecutive successful passes.

drill 49 chest pass 3

Objective: To develop confidence and co-ordination.

Equipment: Three balls between two players.

Description: On the coach's command, player 1 picks up a ball and chest passes to her partner, who catches the ball and puts it on the ground. Player 1 completes three passes and then the roles reverse.

Coaching points: The chest pass is a flat pass used to cover short distances. It is made from chest height using both hands, with the fingers behind the ball. The ball is pushed with the fingertips pointing to the receiver and the player stepping through the pass with either foot. The step brings the hips and legs into the pass and will provide more speed and power.

drill 50 *chest pass 4*

Objective: To practise the chest pass.

Equipment: One ball per team.

Description: Divide the players into teams of eight. Set the teams up in a zigzag formation with approximately 2 m between teams. On the coach's command, the ball is passed up the line using a chest pass.

Coaching points: Younger players will get excited as they become engrossed in the game and will want to unload the ball quickly instead of executing a good pass. If this becomes a problem, tell the players that they are responsible for the ball until the receiver has caught it, so if a pass is dropped or missed then the passer has to retrieve it and run back to make a new pass.

Progression: This drill can be made continuous by asking the players to run to the end of the line after they have passed. If you have two teams, an element of competition can be introduced by setting a distance to be covered and seeing which team can do so the quickest.

drill 51 *shoulder pass 1*

Objective: To develop confidence and co-ordination.

Equipment: One ball between two players.

Description: Players stand approximately 5 m apart. Player 1 has the ball, and player 2 stands with her hands up ready to receive the pass.

Coaching points: This is a flat, hard pass used to cover longer distances. It can be a one- or two-handed pass. Start by establishing the stronger side for each player, that is whether they are left- or right-handed. If they are right-handed, the ball should be held at shoulder height on the right with the right hand behind the ball and vice versa for left-handed players. Players should step forwards as they pass and follow through with their fingers pointing in the direction of the pass, their eye on the receiver and their head up, looking to where they are passing. The step through will bring the big muscles of the hips and legs into the pass to deliver speed and power. Keep everything slow and controlled at first and allow the players to get the feel of the pass.

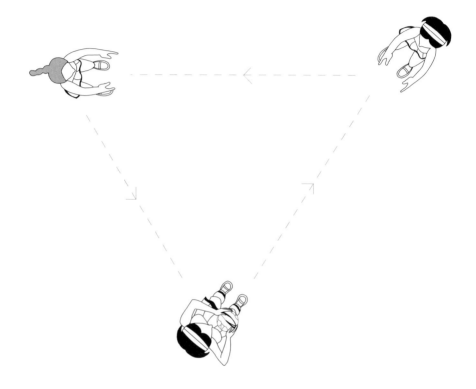

Objective: To practise the shoulder pass.

Equipment: One ball between three players.

Description: Set up the groups in a triangle with approximately 7 m between the players. On the coach's command, the ball is passed anti-clockwise around the triangle using a shoulder pass.

Coaching points: The passing player is responsible for the ball until the receiver has caught it, so if a pass is dropped or missed then the passer has to retrieve it and run back to make a new pass. This will ensure accuracy rather than a quick off-load of the ball.

Objective: To practise the shoulder pass.

Equipment: One ball per team.

Description: Divide the players into teams of eight. Set up the teams in a zigzag formation with approximately 7 m between teams. On the coach's command, the ball is passed up the line using a shoulder pass.

Coaching points: Younger players will get excited as they become engrossed in the drill and will want to unload the ball quickly instead of executing a good pass. If this becomes a problem, tell the players that they are responsible for the ball until the receiver has caught it, so if a pass is dropped or missed then the passer has to retrieve it and run back to make a new pass.

Progression: This drill can be made continuous by asking the players to run to the end of the line after they have passed. If you have two teams, an element of competition can be introduced by setting a distance to be covered and seeing which team manages to do so first.

drill 54 *accurate passing*

Objective: To increase accuracy when passing.

Equipment: One ball between two players and a wall.

Description: Divide the players into pairs. Decide which pass they are practising (chest pass, bounce pass or shoulder pass) and mark several numbered points on a wall, taking into account the type of pass and the size of the players involved. Player 1 starts with the ball facing the wall and player 2 stands behind player 1. Player 2 shouts a number, and player 1 must aim a pass at the corresponding point on the wall and catch the rebound. After five successful passes and catches, swap roles.

Coaching points: Look for accurate passes.

Progression: Vary the type of pass.

drill 55 *the box*

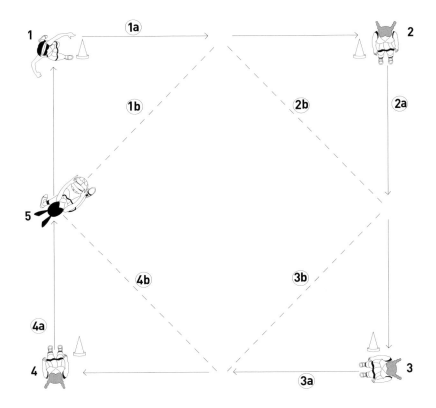

Objective: To practise passing on the move. This drill requires concentration and co-ordination so is only suitable for older, more experienced players.

Equipment: One ball and four cones per group.

Description: Divide the players into groups of five. Use the cones to mark out a square with approximately 7 m sides. Players each stand at a cone. Player 5 stands halfway between cones 4 and 1 with the ball. Player 1 runs towards cone 2 and player 5 passes ahead of her so that the pass will be received at the mid-point between the two cones. Player 5 then runs to the space left at cone 1. As soon as player 1 receives the ball, player 2 runs towards cone 3, player 1 passes to her, then runs on to cone 2 and so on.

Coaching points: This is a complicated drill so walk through the sequence first, then build up the pace. Look for a controlled, balanced landing. Each pass should be accurate and into the space the runner is moving into.

Progression: Vary the type of pass used.

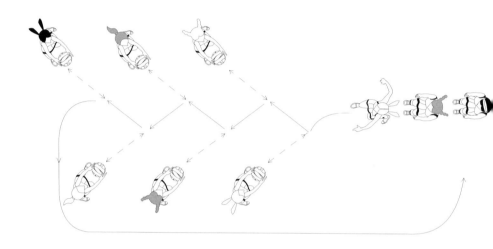

Objective: To improve passing and throwing confidence. Players need to be able to apply the stepping rule confidently.

Equipment: One ball between two players.

Description: Set-up the players with the throwers in a zigzag approximately 5 m apart. The throwers start with a ball each. The remaining players are the workers and form a line at the end of the court. Player 1 starts sprinting towards the first thrower to receive a pass. Thrower 1 passes the ball ahead of player 1, who catches it and returns it to the thrower. Player 1 then pushes off quickly and changes direction to head straight to the next thrower, who passes the ball as above. This is continued until all the throwers have passed.

Coaching points: Look for the players sprinting hard into the space to receive the ball and a controlled, balanced landing. Each pass should be accurate and into the space the runner is moving into. Look for an accurate, balanced return pass.

Progression: Vary the type of pass used.

Objective: To practise throwing the ball ahead of a running player and catching a ball when on the run. This is a more advanced ball skills drill and is only suitable for older players.

Equipment: One ball between two players.

Description: In pairs, players stand approximately 2 m apart. Player 2 is the thrower and starts with the ball. Player 1 runs to the side and player 2 throws the ball ahead of player 1, who catches the ball, pivots and throws the ball back to player 2. Player 1 returns to face player 2, then runs to the other side and the steps are repeated. After five passes to each side, swap over roles.

Coaching points: Look for passes ahead of the running player to ensure they run onto the ball and don't have to reach backwards or stop to catch the pass. The landing should be balanced and controlled and the pivoting foot should remain still.

Progression: Vary the pass, introducing high or lob passes for example.

Objective: To develop passing confidence and teamwork.

Equipment: One ball and one set of bibs.

Description: Divide the players into two teams. Use one third of the court as the working area. Team A is the attacking team and starts with the ball. Team B is defending and aims to gain possession by intercepting passes. Once team B gains possession, the roles reverse. Possession also changes if the ball is dropped, the players break the footwork rule or the players go out of the working area. Each team gets a point if they link together a set number of consecutive passes or intercept the ball.

Coaching points: Look for and encourage short, sharp movements when getting free from defending players. Encourage players to run towards the ball to receive a pass rather than running away from it.

Progression: When players are more confident at using the whole space, restrict the pass so that a player cannot pass back to the player she received the ball from.

drill 59 *fireball*

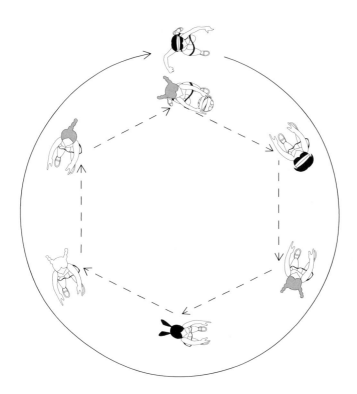

Objective: To develop passing confidence, quick reactions and balanced movement. Players need to be able to concentrate on the passing and be able to throw and catch, so this drill is not suitable for very young players.

Equipment: One ball.

Description: One player is the runner. The rest of the group stand in a circle. The aim is for the runner to sprint around the outside of the circle and return to her space before the ball is passed around the circle by the other players. The drill starts on the coach's whistle and continues with each player taking a turn as the runner.

Coaching points: Don't make the circle too big. Look for quick, accurate passing – the ball should be controlled, but should also leave the players' hands quickly, as if it were on fire! The runners should use quick, little steps to move around the circle – encourage them to keep their heads up and look where they are going.

Progression: The runner can move in the opposite direction to the ball. Introduce another runner and another ball – not for the faint hearted!

drill 60 all change!

Objective: To develop confidence and improve accuracy and speed of passing.

Equipment: Four cones and one ball between four players.

Description: Set out the cones in a square with 2 m sides. The players stand in position, one at each cone. Player 1 starts with the ball. On the coach's whistle, the players pass the ball in turn, player 1 to player 2 to player 3 and so on, using a chest pass. Whenever the coach blows the whistle, the ball should change direction. If the coach shouts 'all change', all players must swap places and move to a different corner of the square. Once the players are back in position at a different corner, the ball begins to be passed around the players again. The first group to pass the ball around their square 20 times without dropping it is the winner.

Coaching points: Look for accurate passing with the players being balanced before making the pass, with their feet and fingers pointing in the direction they are passing.

Progression: Increase the size of the square and vary the type of pass used.

ATTACKING AND DEFENDING

Although there are defending (GK, GD, WD) and attacking positions (GS, GA, WA, C) on a netball team, all with definite roles, all players need to be able to adopt both an attacking and a defensive role within a game, depending on the situation. With younger players, the change between the two is often hard as it relies on the players understanding the flow of the game and being able to 'read' the play to anticipate what will happen next. These are advanced skills and will develop with experience and confidence.

The aim of this next section is to develop awareness of the attacking and defending roles and responsibilities, and when players should adopt a particular role. Getting a young player to recognise that their team has lost possession and they must now defend, that is mark their partner to try to stop them getting free to receive a pass or mark the ball with their hands high, is a huge achievement.

In addition, this section aims to develop controlled aggression, the desire to 'win' the ball, and the determination to gain possession and never give up – qualities that all good netballers possess.

key coaching points

1 Defenders need to have controlled, balanced footwork to be able to move quickly in all directions. They also need to be able to jump! It is surprising how many players seem to have their feet rooted to the ground, so encourage young players to jump and meet the ball whatever their size.
2 Defenders need to keep going even when it appears that their efforts are wasted. This is hard for young players; however, perseverance is a key quality for defenders. Try to ensure players understand how their efforts are having a positive impact on the game by putting off the attack or forcing mistakes, and encourage them to keep going.
3 The ultimate aim of the attackers is to score goals! Developing confidence in young players will help them work together as a team and improve their awareness of the space, each other and the passes they can use.

golden rule

All players should be determined to get the ball and never give up chasing – it is surprising how many loose balls on court are reached or how many balls are prevented from going out of court by the dogged, enthusiastic player who chases every ball and never gives up!

As my netball teacher used to say, 'the netball court is the only place I want to see you snatching the ball!' A good habit to get into.

drill 61 _scramble_

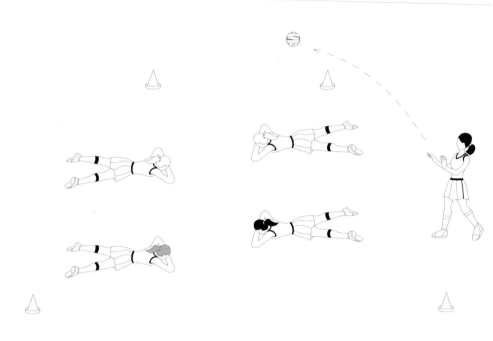

Objective: To encourage quick reactions to a loose ball – important for all players!

Equipment: One ball and four cones per group.

Description: Divide the players into groups of 3. Mark out a square with 5 m sides using the cones. One player in each group is the feeder and the others are the scramblers. The scramblers start by lying down on their stomachs in the square with their eyes closed. (If it is too wet or cold to lie down, players may crouch down low with their eyes closed.) The feeder throws the ball in the air and shouts 'scramble'. The scramblers must jump up and scramble for the ball. The player who retrieves the ball throws the ball for the next scramble.

Coaching points: There needs to be space between the groups to avoid collisions and confusion. Encourage players to snatch the ball in to their chest to gain possession. Players must try to avoid barging each other out of the way.

Progression: Increase the size of the working area and combine two groups. Use two balls.

drill 62 *jump*

Objective: To practise competing for the ball in the air.

Equipment: One ball between three players.

Description: Divide the players into groups of three. The two working players stand side by side with their shoulders just touching. The feeder stands with the ball 2 m away, facing the players. The feeder throws the ball to the players, alternating between high and low passes. The players compete to see who can retrieve it first.

Coaching points: This drill can get quite competitive with some players, so encourage them not to barge each other out of the way! Look for players being 'ready' – up on their toes and watching the ball.

drill 63 *tipping*

Objective: To practise jumping to tip the ball in the air.

Equipment: One ball between two players.

Description: Divide the players into pairs. Player 1 is working. Player 2 stands balancing the ball high above her head in one hand. Player 1 takes a short run-up and jumps high, aiming to tip the ball off the hand of her partner. She should aim to tip the ball and not knock the arm or hand of the other player, which would be contact in a game situation. If the ball is tipped, player 1 should try to catch it, or retrieve it quickly. Swap roles after five attempts.

Coaching points: It is useful to pair players of similar heights to make this drill even. Look for a controlled run-up and a correctly timed jump to tip the ball only. Encourage player 1 to chase the tipped ball and catch it if possible.

Progression: If the ball is tipped, both players should try to retrieve the ball – watch out for contact!

drill 64 *shadowing*

Objective: To encourage concentration and develop ball awareness.

Equipment: One ball.

Description: Arrange the players in a circle facing inwards, with the coach standing in the centre with the ball. The players start 'fast feet' movements on the spot and react to the moves that the coach makes, shadowing or mirroring all of his or her moves. To start with, the coach simply moves the ball to the left, right, front, up, down and so on, and the players all copy by moving their arms to the same place as the ball.

Coaching points: Keep the movements coming thick and fast once the group has got the hang of the drill. Don't allow fatigue to lead to sloppiness. Short, sharp bursts interspersed with rests is much better. Players must keep fast feet throughout.

Progression: To progress, the coach can now toss the ball up in the air and the players must react by jumping up to 'catch' the ball. The coach can even drop the ball to either side and the players must stoop to 'collect' it.

drill 65 *marking a player*

Objective: To introduce one-on-one marking.

Equipment: Two cones between two players.

Description: Place the cones approximately 3 m apart. The attacker stands in the middle of the cones with the defender standing in front, facing the same way. The defender's shoulders need to be at a slight angle to enable her to look over her shoulder at the attacker as well as at the ball. The attacker moves between the cones using side steps, changing direction at random. The defender aims to stick closely to the attacker, copying her movements.

Coaching points: One-on-one marking is where the defender stays close to the attacker, to restrict her movement and to intercept the pass. The defender should mark her partner without contacting her. The attacker should be on her toes, with her weight forwards, using short, sharp movements.

Progression: Increase the working area and allow the attacker to move freely.

Objective: To improve confidence with one-on-one marking of a player.

Equipment: One ball and two cones between three players.

Description: Place the cones approximately 3 m apart. The attacker stands in the middle of the cones with the defender in front, facing the same way. The defender's shoulders need to be at a slight angle to enable her to look over her shoulder at the attacker as well as at the ball. The thrower stands opposite the attacker approximately 3 m away. The attacker must dodge to get free and receive a pass from the thrower. The defender aims to stick closely to the attacker and intercept the pass.

Coaching points: The attacker should be on her toes, with her weight forwards, using short, sharp movements. Encourage the attacker to point to where she wants to receive the ball. The defender should keep her head up, glancing over her shoulder to keep an eye on the attacker and also looking forwards to keep an eye on the thrower.

Progression: Increase the working area and allow the attacker to move freely.

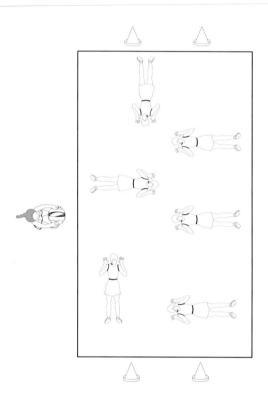

Objective: To encourage quick reactions and quick decision-making.

Equipment: One ball, four cones and one set of bibs per seven players.

Description: Using a third of the court, set up the cones approximately 1 m apart in the middle of the side lines – these are the goal areas. One player in each group is the feeder; the others are the scramblers and need to be split into two teams. The scramblers lie on their stomachs. The feeder throws the ball in the air and shouts 'scramble'. The scramblers must jump up and scramble for the ball. The team that retrieves the ball becomes the attacking team and must then pass the ball between themselves, working towards their goal area. A goal is scored when the ball is caught by a team player standing between the cones of their goal area.

Coaching points: Encourage players to snatch the ball in to their chest to gain possession. Players must try to avoid barging each other out of the way! Encourage teams to react quickly to the situation and move into attacking or defensive mode.

Progression: The defenders can earn points for intercepting the ball.

drill 68 *the faker*

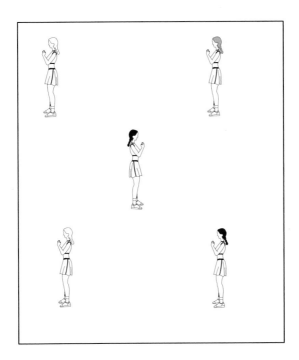

Objective: To improve peripheral vision and practise faking the direction of a pass. This drill is only suitable for older players.

Equipment: Players, one third of the court.

Description: Players jog around the playing area. On the coach's whistle, they stop and get into the correct position to make a pass – feet shoulder width apart, knees bent and head up. Players must have two people in their vision without making eye contact with anyone. If they make eye contact with anyone they are 'out'.

Coaching points: It is best to give each player two or three lives as young players like to be 'in' and playing, rather than having to sit out. This skill is not often included in training sessions for younger players as it is considered an advanced skill. However, the ability to deceive the opposition when attacking is a powerful skill to use in a game and it is useful to introduce this to players at an early age.

Objective: To practise faking a pass to confuse a defender, and to encourage players to watch the ball and expect a pass even if they are not being looked at.

Equipment: Players, one third of the court.

Description: Players jog around the playing area. On the coach's whistle, they get into the correct position to make a pass – feet shoulder width apart, knees bent and head up. A feeder stands in the middle of the group with the ball. At the coach's whistle, the feeder must have two players in her vision without looking directly at anyone, and should pass the ball to one of these players. If the feeder makes eye contact with anyone they are 'out'. Whoever receives the ball becomes the feeder.

Coaching points: Use two balls with two passers if the group is large. It is best to give each player two or three lives as young players like to be 'in' and playing. Players need to keep their heads up to be able to use their peripheral vision.

Progression: Include a defender to mark the receiver of the ball, who must get two other players in her vision and pass the ball to one of them.

drill 70 *the triangle*

Objective: To practise 'reading' a pass.

Equipment: One ball between four players.

Description: Three players stand in a triangle 3–4 m apart. One player, the thrower, starts with the ball. The fourth player is the defender and stands opposite the thrower, between and a little in front of the other two players. The thrower makes a chest pass to either receiver and the defender must try to intercept it. The receiver should land correctly and return the ball to the thrower using a chest pass. Rotate roles after five clean interceptions.

Coaching points: The distance between the players can be varied according to the skill and size of the defender to ensure she has a realistic chance of making the interception. The defender should react to the ball, not to the thrower's eyes. The receivers should make a definite move to get free and receive the pass without contacting the defender. Look for quick, accurate chest passes. Ensure the distance between players is maintained throughout the drill.

Progression: Increase the distance between the receivers.

Objective: To practise timing a run to intercept a pass.

Equipment: One ball between three players.

Description: Players 1 and 2 stand approximately 3 m apart and pass the ball between each other using a chest pass. The defender stands behind player 2 and must run around her to intercept the ball, then returns the ball to the throwers. Rotate roles frequently.

Coaching points: The defender must time her move around the player in order to catch the ball. Look for the defender moving around the player without causing contact and landing in a balanced, controlled way. The defender should move around both sides of the players. Look for good quality chest passes at all times.

Progression: Vary the type of pass used.

drill 72 *marking relay*

①

C A B D

②

C A B

Objective: To practise passing and defending skills.

Equipment: Two cones and one ball between four players.

Description: Place the cones 3–4 m apart. Players A and C start at cone 1. A has the ball. Players B and D start at cone 2. Player A passes the ball to player B using a chest pass and runs to follow the ball, defending the return pass to player C with high arms. Once the second pass is made, player A runs to the back of the line behind player D. Continue until all players have had three runs each, then stop the drill and reaffirm the objectives and key skills.

Coaching points: Look for accurate passes at all times. Encourage players to sprint after the ball and immediately adopt a defending stance with their arms high and fingers spread wide. This will make them as tall as possible, making it hard for the next pass to be thrown accurately.

Progression: Increase the distance between the players and vary the type of pass used.

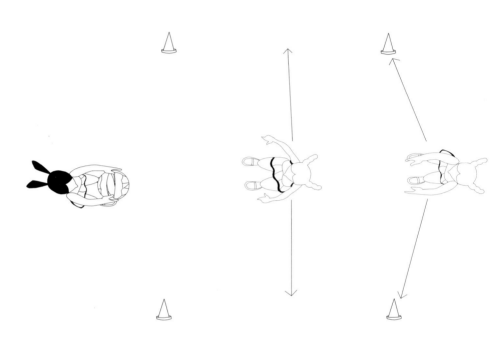

Objective: To practise passing, receiving, getting free and defending the ball.

Equipment: One ball and four cones between three players.

Description: Mark out a small square with the cones, large enough to allow some sideways movement but small enough to restrict the players. The three players stand in the middle of the square in a straight line. Players A and C, the attackers, pass the ball to each other. Player B, the defender, stands in between the attackers and tries to intercept the pass. Rotate the players frequently.

Coaching points: The attackers should use quick, short side steps to move into a space and make it easier for their partner to make an accurate pass. Encourage the defender to mark the ball using high arms. The defender can choose to defend only one attacker or both.

Progression: This simple drill can be advanced by introducing another defender. With two defenders marking the ball by facing their attacking player, the attackers will need to move quickly into a space to receive a pass.

drill 74 *piggies in the middle*

Objective: To develop confidence and quick reactions.

Equipment: One ball between seven players.

Description: Form each group into a circle with two players in the centre. The remaining players pass the ball across the circle using various types of passes. The players in the middle try to intercept the ball. Change players after a certain number of passes have been made. The 'piggies in the middle' keep score of how many touches (1 point), knock-downs (3 points) or catches (10 points) they make. At the end, the player with the most points is the winner.

Coaching points: Look for quick, accurate passes. Defenders should be on their toes, using short, sharp steps to keep moving to intercept.

Progression: Introduce passing without speaking. Receivers signal for the ball (left, right, up, down). Passers can experiment with eye-feints, looking at one player and passing to another, and fake passes.

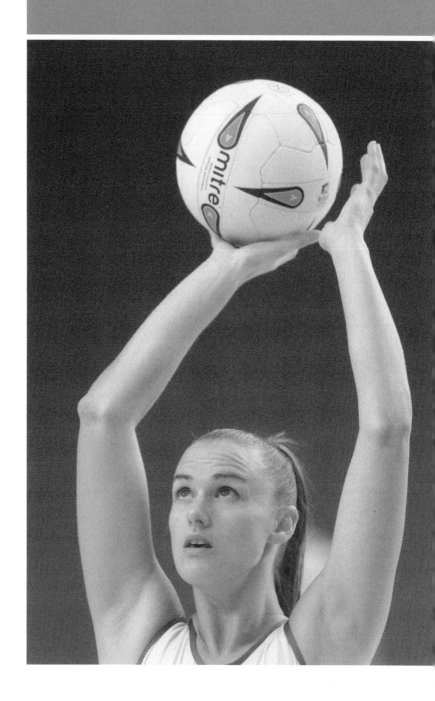

SHOOTING

Shooting is a very specific skill requiring accuracy, good balance, control of movement and confidence in the circle. Most young players want to be goal shooter or goal attack, but players are often complacent in these positions, not fully understanding the complexity of the skills required to be a successful shooter.

A good GS and GA have good awareness of space within the circle and the ability to take control of that space, maintaining focus on a consistent shooting action while under pressure from the defence. For very young players, these are very difficult skills to master. There are some basic drills young players can practise to give them a good understanding of the role of GS and GA, which can be developed as their confidence and experience grow.

In all the shooting drills to follow there are some key coaching points to consider and skills to encourage. The following points are applicable to all shooters; bear in mind it may take some time for younger players to get to grips with them. The height of the post should be lowered to 2 m.

- Young shooters have five seconds to turn and shoot, and the first thing they need to be sure of is correct balance. Feet should be shoulder width apart and toes should be pointing towards the net before a shot is attempted.
- The power and energy for the shot comes from the floor, so the knees should be bent as if the shooter is about to jump into the air. The back should be straight and the head up.
- The ball should be held on the fingertips above the head supported by the other hand, not out in front. The grip should be light, just enough to propel the ball into the net.
- Shooters should focus on a point at the back rather than at the front of the ring, aiming high for the back of the net. This is because if the shot is short it could still fall in!
- Shooters should aim before taking the shot and bend their elbows and knees when ready to shoot.
- The ball should be released at the same time as the shooter straightens her legs. The shooter should move her arms as little as possible, and use a flick of the wrist to add backspin.
- As the shooter prepares to release the ball, she should drop her hands back behind her head. This is the most accurate way to control the direction of the ball.
- The shot should end with the shooter standing on tiptoes with her arms following through towards the ring.

And the golden rule in the circle, for both attackers and defenders: always follow the shot in case it misses – rebounds represent a second chance! Take every opportunity to reaffirm this to form good habits.

Objective: To introduce and practise the correct shooting action.

Equipment: Goal post and a good supply of balls.

Description: The shooter should stand facing the goalpost with her feet parallel and shoulder width apart and her body well balanced, holding the ball on the fingers of one hand directly above her head with a high, extended arm position, the elbow close to the ear and pointing towards the ring. The fingers of the non-shooting hand are just used to support the ball. The shooting wrist should drop back slightly behind the head while the knees bend. Drive up with the legs and release the ball from just above the head with a flick of the wrist, following through to the target with the fingers. This wrist 'snap' gives the ball backspin and allows the ball to travel in a higher arc, increasing the chances of success.

Coaching points: Ask the shooter where she is aiming, what she sees, hears and feels when the ball goes well.

Progression: Set cones around the goal circle to practise shooting from different positions.

Objective: To practise controlling forward movement, getting into a balanced shooting position and maintaining correct shooting action technique.

Equipment: One ball and one goalpost between two players.

Description: One player is shooting, the other is the feeder, standing on the circle edge. The shooter starts on the opposite side of the circle just inside the circle edge, facing the post. When ready, the shooter sprints into the space underneath the post and the feeder passes her the ball. The shooter should jump to catch the ball and land two-footed, then attempt a shot.

Coaching points: Look for a fast, controlled sprint into a space by the shooter and a balanced, two-footed landing. The shooter only has five seconds to shoot once she has received the ball, so the more accurate the pass and the more controlled the landing the better. Look for correct shooting technique and a balanced shooting position.

Progression: Vary the starting positions of the feeder and shooter.

drill 77 *dirty dungeons*

Objective: To practise shooting. This drill works best with older players who have more control of the shooting action.

Equipment: Two balls.

Description: Divide the players into two teams. Each team has one ball. Each player gets a maximum of one shot per turn. If they are successful with this shot, they stay in the game; if they miss, they must stand in the dungeon (next to the post). Any player standing in the dungeon can be released back into the game by one of their team scoring a goal. Once everybody on one team is in the dungeon the other team wins. For younger players, a target circle on a wall can be used instead of posts. This provides an easier target, but players will still be able to practise a balanced position and the correct shooting action.

Coaching points: Look for correct shooting technique and a balanced position.

Progression: Add a defender to mark the shot.

drill 78 *under the post*

Objective: To practise getting free of a defender to receive the ball under the post.

Equipment: One ball and one goalpost between three players.

Description: Divide the players into groups of three. The feeder stands on the circle edge with the ball. The shooter and defender start opposite the feeder, with the defender between the ball and the shooter. The shooter sprints into the space under the post to receive the ball, aiming to get there before the defender. The defender can try to intercept the ball or tip it to prevent the shooter receiving the ball.

Coaching points: Look for a fast, controlled sprint by the shooter. The defender can hold back at first if the shooter is having difficulty receiving the pass.

Progression: Introduce a dodge for the shooter to get free of the defender and move into a space under the post.

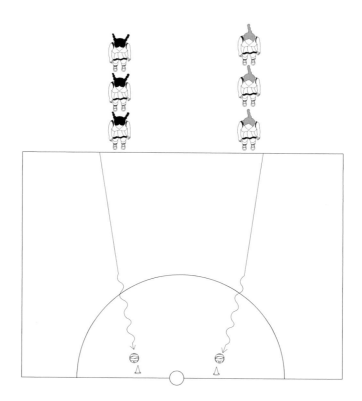

Objective: To practise a balanced shooting position following a move into the circle.

Equipment: Two balls, two cones and one goalpost.

Description: Divide the players into two teams. The balls are placed by the cones on the edge of the circle. Each team starts on a line facing the nearest goalpost. One at a time from each team, players move towards the goalpost using different footwork, such as jogging, skipping or cross-over stepping. The coach or players can decide on the footwork pattern to be used. Once they reach the cone, the players pick up the ball and shoot a goal or have three shots at goal (whichever occurs first), then replace the ball by the cone and run back to the starting line. The next player on their team then begins the drill. Each player needs to complete three trips to the post. The first team to finish is the winner.

Coaching points: Look for balanced, controlled movement into the circle, the correct shooting position and a balanced shooting action.

Progression: With older players, you can add a defender. Alternatively, add a feeder to pass the ball to the shooters as they enter the circle.

drill 80 *rebound and snatch*

Objective: To encourage young players to chase a loose ball and catch the rebound.

Equipment: One ball and a wall between three players.

Description: Two players are working and one is the feeder. The two working players start facing the wall approximately 2 m away from it. The feeder has the ball and stands slightly behind and to one side of the working players. The feeder throws the ball at the wall, aiming above the heads of the other two players. The working players compete to catch the ball on the rebound, or, if it bounces to retrieve it. A player gets 2 points for catching the ball on the rebound and 1 point if the ball is retrieved after a bounce. Rotate the players after a certain number of throws and compare points at the end of the drill to see who is the winner.

Coaching points: Look for determination to get to the ball first. Watch out for too much contact, but encourage players to snatch the ball to gain possession.

Progression: Use a target circle on the wall for the feeder to aim at.

drill 81 *the rebound 1*

Objective: To practise following the shot and catching the rebound. This drill is aimed at younger players.

Equipment: One ball and a wall between two players.

Description: Chalk a target circle on the wall approximately 3 m high. One player is the shooter and the other is the defender. They start side by side facing the wall approximately 2 m away from it. The shooter should try to 'shoot' the ball into the target circle, using the correct shooting position and technique. On the rebound, both players should try to catch or retrieve the ball. A player gets 2 points for catching the ball on the rebound and 1 point if the ball is retrieved after a bounce.

Coaching points: Look for the correct shooting technique and position. Players should be determined to get to the ball first. Watch out for too much contact, but encourage players to snatch the ball to gain possession.

Progression: The defender can mark the shooter while she is making the shot and will need to turn to catch the rebound after the shot has been made.

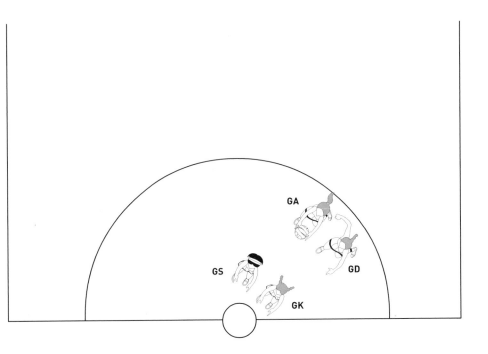

Objective: To practise following the shot and catching the rebound in the circle.

Equipment: One ball and a goalpost between four players.

Description: The GS, GK, GA and GD start in the circle as shown. The shooters take it in turns to take a shot at goal with the defenders marking the shot. The shooter who isn't shooting holds their position under the post waiting for the rebound. The shooter should follow the shot to try and catch the rebound. The defenders should also try for the rebound. Any loose balls should be chased and retrieved. Swap roles frequently.

Coaching points: Look for correct shooting technique and position. The defenders marking the shot will need to turn quickly to try to catch the rebound or retrieve any loose balls. Players should be determined to get to the ball first. Watch out for too much contact but encourage players to snatch the ball to gain possession.

drill 83 hold that space

Objective: To practise holding the space behind a player to receive an overhead pass. This can be used under the post or on back line or side line throw-ins.

Equipment: One ball between three players.

Description: One player is the feeder, one is the attacker and one is the defender. The feeder starts with the ball (this position would be WA, GA or C in a game). The attacker stands behind the defender, slightly sideways, with one foot behind the other, and indicates to receive the ball behind her. The feeder should throw an overhead pass to land behind the attacker, who should hold her position until the ball is overhead and then take one step back to catch the ball.

Coaching points: The attacker should use her body to shield the space in which she wants to receive the ball from the defender. If the attacker moves backwards too early the defender will be able to step back and make an easy interception.

Progression: Vary the position of the feeder so the attacker has to receive the pass from different directions.

GAME SCENARIOS

the centre pass

These drills introduce the basics of a netball game to the younger players, and include the development of quick reactions to the whistle, and different options for a centre pass for more experienced and confident players.

Let the players try out all the different centre-court positions to help them understand the different roles and responsibilities of each. Most young players adopt a very regimented approach to starting the game and the centre pass, standing in the same position every time, moving in the same way, and throwing the ball to the same person. Encourage players to try out different starting points along the third line, different moves into a space to catch the ball and different positions to receive the centre pass.

The starting position at each centre pass is crucial for attacking players. The WA and GA should try to get into a position along the third line they are happy with, preferably on the outside of their defending player. Although WA usually starts on the left and GA on the right, this doesn't have to be true every time. However, if the players stand too close to the side line, this will restrict the space available for them to run into to receive the pass. If the WA and GA stand too close together in the centre of the third line it makes it easy for the defenders to mark them and stop the run to receive the pass. Defenders WD and GD should try to make things as difficult for their attacking partners as possible by dominating the space along the third line, forcing the WA and GA to take up a position that is easier to mark and reducing the space into which they can run.

Objective: To introduce and practise the centre-pass movement and improve reactions to the umpire's whistle.

Equipment: One ball and three cones between three players.

Description: Set up players as shown using the cones to mark a triangular working area. The centre starts with the ball. On the coach's whistle, the other two players run in a straight line; the centre must pass the ball to one of the players. Rotate the roles frequently.

Coaching points: Encourage both the centre and the players to react quickly to the whistle as if it were the start of a game. The players must sprint into the space, pushing off on one foot and using their arms to help keep balance and speed. Hands should be ready to receive the ball. The centre should pass the ball into the space the players are running into, not behind them!

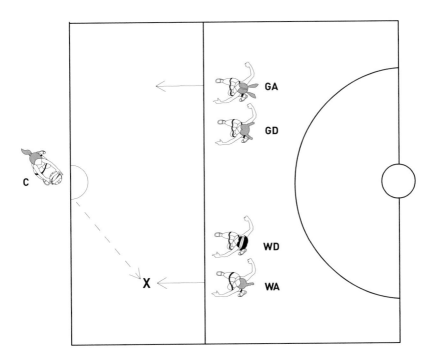

Objective: To introduce and practise attacking centre passes.

Equipment: One ball and half the court between eight players.

Description: Set up the players as shown, as if starting a game. The centre pass must go to the WA. On the coach's whistle, the WA runs straight to receive the pass at X. The GA should also run into the centre third as if to receive the pass. The defenders start the drill in position, but should stay still to allow the WA and GA to run into the space easily. The second pass should go to the GA.

Coaching points: The WA should sprint into the space to meet the ball at X. If the WA runs diagonally towards the side line, she will reduce the space available and make it easier for the WD to intercept the ball. Encourage quick reactions to the whistle.

Progression: The centre can choose who to throw to, WA or GA. The defenders can try to intercept the ball and mark their attacking partner. Encourage older players (WA and GA) to try out different starting points along the line.

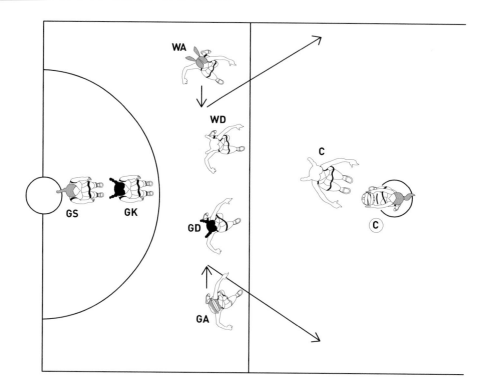

Objective: To practise dodging to get free to receive the centre pass.

Equipment: One ball and half the court between eight players.

Description: This drill provides an alternative way of getting free for the centre pass. On the coach's whistle, the WA and GA dodge to get free and sprint into the centre third. The defenders should stand still at first. The pass can go to either player chosen by the C, but with younger players the coach may need to indicate where the pass should go at first.

Coaching points: The dodge should be a definite movement, controlled, quick and balanced. Look for the WA and GA pushing off on their outside foot and using their shoulders to help perform the dodge and make the move quick and controlled.

Progression: Introduce the defenders. Encourage them to try to stick with their players and intercept the ball.

WD

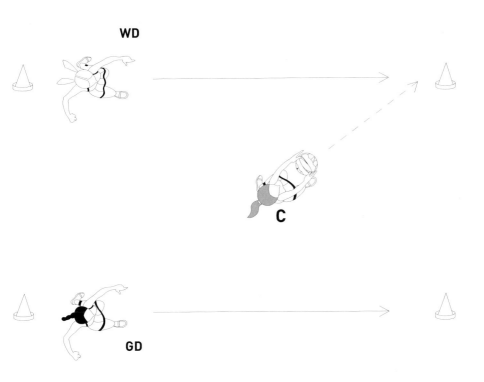

C

GD

Objective: To introduce using the WD and GD to receive the centre pass. This drill is aimed at older, more experienced players.

Equipment: One ball and four cones between three players.

Description: The idea behind this drill is to reproduce the centre court positions at a centre pass for the WD, GD and C. Divide the players into groups of three and use the cones to mark out a working area approximately 5 m square. The C stands in the middle of the square with the ball. The WD and GD start at the cones as shown, standing behind the C. On the coach's whistle the WD and GD sprint in a straight line towards the opposite cones. The C should pass the ball to either player, aiming for them to catch the ball at the cone in front of them.

Coaching points: Look for the WD and GD sprinting towards the second cone. The C must wait for the players to pass her before throwing the ball.

Progression: Introduce a WA and GA to mark the WD and GD. The WA and GA should stand outside the WD and GD, sprinting with them to try to intercept the ball.

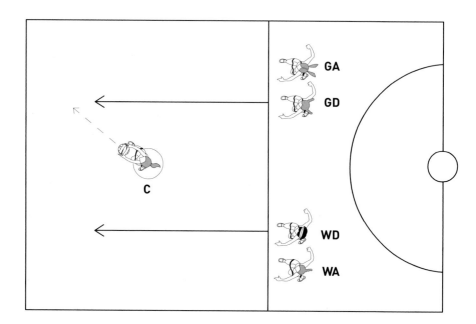

Objective: To practice WD/GD receiving a centre pass in an attacking position.

Equipment: One ball and half the court between five players.

Description: Set up the players as shown. The C starts with the ball and should be facing away from the WD and GD. On the coach's whistle, WD and GD sprint in a straight line, aiming to receive the ball as close to the attacking third line as possible. Alternate the players receiving the pass. Restrict defending players (WA and GA) until the WD and GD are more confident.

Coaching points: To receive a centre pass without a good chance of the ball being intercepted, the WD and GD should position themselves inside their defending players ready for the centre pass. It is worth letting the WD and GD try to receive the centre pass having started on the outside of their defending players; this puts the C under more pressure to make an accurate pass and makes it easier to intercept by the WA and GA.

Progression: Encourage the defending players to try for the interception. Look for the player receiving the pass to make a second pass to either the WA or GA.

the throw-in

The player taking the throw-in depends on where on the court the ball goes out of play. Younger players don't always think about the positioning and spacing on court and are keen to take throw-ins to be part of the game, wherever the throw-in may be. However, if a player taking the throw-in is out of position on the court, it will have an impact on the next sequence of passes in the game. Encouraging young players to think about the 'correct' person to take the throw-in is a good habit to get into.

The following drills enable players to practise set moves for a variety of throw-ins, although the combinations are endless and players will need to be encouraged to be flexible and think about the best options available in each situation.

Coaching points to consider when taking a throw-in

1 The player must stand with one foot up to but not touching the side line of the court. This indicates to the umpire that the player is ready to make the pass. If the player's feet are touching the line, a free throw-in will be given to the opposite team. An umpire may also penalise a player who is standing too far away from the line – this is not likely to happen with younger players, but good positioning is worth encouraging.

2 The player taking the throw-in should look to pass the ball in to an attacking or forward position on court. There may be occasions when the throw-in will need to be passed backwards if players are not free, but players should be encouraged to look forwards.

3 All players must be on court before the pass is taken. This also applies to members of the opposite team who may have gone off court to retrieve the ball. If a player takes the throw-in without waiting for that player to get back on court, a free pass will be given to the opposite team.

4 Players on court should be ready to receive the pass, either holding a space to run into or ready to dodge and get free.

5 Players defending a throw-in should be 1 m away from the side line to avoid giving away a penalty pass.

6 Any back line throw-in taken in the defensive goal third should be taken by the GK.

7 Never throw a back line pass across the circle, as if the pass is intercepted it will give the attacking team an immediate shot at goal.

The player taking the throw-in can decide whether to take the throw-in quickly or take more time. There may be an advantage if the throw-in is taken quickly, for example to get the ball into the circle to an unmarked GA or GS. There may also be advantages to taking more time to prepare before taking the throw-in, for example if team players are out of position and need time to recover on court.

This may be too complicated for younger players, who, as we have already mentioned, tend not to think about spacing and timing of passes on court. It is something that coaches can introduce to more experienced young players.

Objective: For the WD and GD to practise receiving a back line throw-in taken in the circle.

Equipment: One ball and one third of the court between five players.

Description: The defensive back line pass is easy in terms of who takes the throw-in, as it will always be the GK wherever the ball goes out of court. The GK starts with the ball standing on the back line. The other players start in the positions as shown above. The WD and GD should hold their positions on the edge of the circle, making it harder for the WA and GA to mark their free side. When ready, the GK should step up to the line as if to take the throw-in. The WD or GD should aim to receive the pass at the edge of the circle, shielding the ball from the WA or GA with their bodies.

Coaching points: Encourage the WD and GD to hold the space on the edge of the circle. Any movement before the pass will give an advantage to the defender.

Progression: The GD or WD should be ready for the next pass.

drill 90 side line throw-in

Objective: To practise a side line throw-in in the defensive third.

Equipment: One ball and one third of the court.

Description: In this situation the GK should take the throw-in. The WD or GD should aim to receive the pass. With younger players, the coach may need to dictate which player should receive the pass and alternate. WD and GD should dodge to get free of their marker or hold a space to run into.

Coaching points: Encourage the players to hold their space and resist moving up the court to help receive the pass, which will cause crowding.

Progression: The GK should decide which player to pass to depending on who is in the best position to receive the pass.

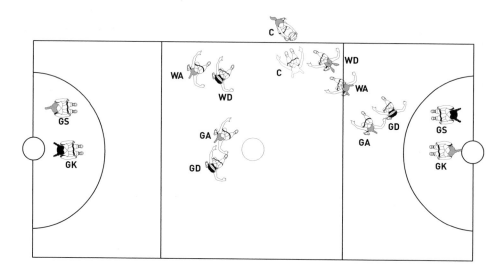

Objective: To practise a throw-in in the centre court. The aim is to encourage players to decide who will receive the throw-in and avoid crowding around the ball.

Equipment: One ball and the whole court.

Description: The coach should vary the position of the throw-in. Let the players play out the side line pass, aiming to maintain an attacking position.

Coaching points: The coach must ensure that a clear pass is given and that the player receiving the throw-in makes a definite move to receive the ball. The other players should avoid crowding and look to receive the next pass. Encourage lots of communication and stop the drill if players do crowd the ball. Walk them through the moves if needed.

Progression: Vary the player taking the throw-in and receiving the pass. Encourage the players to take responsibility for deciding who will take the throw-in and receive the pass, rather than the coach dictating this all the time.

attacking sequences

The following game scenarios practise attacking sequences working in the centre and goal-shooting third. They concentrate on the role of the attacking players and provide typical set piece situations. Sequences for the defence are covered later.

It is useful for young players to try out all the positions even if they already think they are a born GA. This gives players a better understanding of the different roles in the netball team, the responsibilities of each position and the difficulties faced by each one. Also, unless a player has played a position in a game situation, it is difficult for them to make an informed decision about whether they want to play that position or not. Excellent netballers can play in a variety of positions. Versatility is the key – encourage young players to try different positions and have fun in the process.

Key coaching point

When feeding the ball into the circle, the WA and C should work together aiming to have one player at the top of the circle – see diagram.

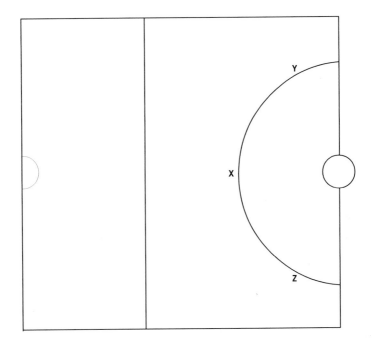

X is the top of the circle – a key attacking position. WA or C should aim to get to the top of the circle which then allows them to pass the ball to either side of the circle or to feed the ball into the shooters.

If C is holding the space at the top of the circle, WA should take up position at Y or Z and vice versa. This gives the attacking team a strong position controlling the space around the circle edge.

drill 92 *to the circle*

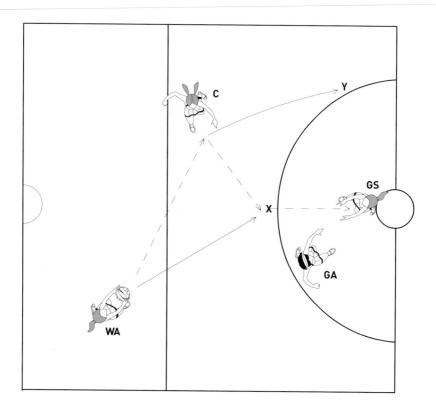

Objective: For GA and GS to practise working in the circle together, focusing on space awareness and control of space.

Equipment: One ball and one third of the court between four players.

Description: This drill does not include defenders in order to let the attacking players gain confidence in the use of space in the attacking third. The GS should hold the space under the post while the WA starts with the ball in the centre third as if she has just received a centre pass. The C and WA pass the ball to the circle edge, aiming for one player to reach X and the other Y or Z. The ball should then be fed into the circle to the GA or GS, who should try a shot.

Coaching points: Encourage the players to communicate with each other and make definite moves into space. There should be little hesitation between passes. Stop the sequence if the game breaks down and encourage players to avoid crowding the ball. Shooters should adopt the correct shooting position and use correct technique.

Progression: Aim to get the ball into the circle with the fewest number of passes.

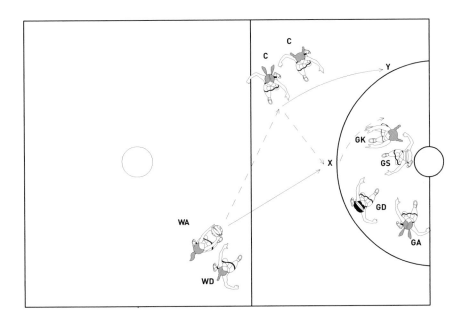

Objective: To introduce GD and GK to the GA and GS working in the circle, getting free to receive a pass and practising awareness and control of space.

Equipment: One ball and the attacking third of the court between eight players.

Description: Defending players should all mark their partners, intercepting passes where possible. GS should hold the space under the post. WA starts with the ball in the centre third, as if a centre pass has just been received. The attacking players pass the ball to reach the circle edge, aiming for one player to reach X and the other Y or Z. The ball should be fed into the circle for the GA or GS to try a shot.

Coaching points: Encourage the attacking players to communicate and make definite moves to get free. Stop the sequence if the game breaks down and constantly encourage players to avoid crowding the ball. If the ball is intercepted, the defenders get one point and the drill restarts.

Progression: Aim to get the ball into the circle with the fewest number of passes.

defensive sequences

The following game scenarios provide some basic drills for defenders working in the centre and defensive goal third. They concentrate on the role of the defending players and typical set piece situations.

Remember, versatility is the key – encourage young players to try different positions in defence as well as in attack and have fun in the process.

Key coaching points

1 A defender should always try to catch the ball – if a player can get one hand to a ball to hit it away from the attacker, she could catch the ball and gain possession.

2 All players will need to be able to defend at certain times in a game – it is as important for a WA, GA and GS to be able to defend the ball, defend their space and mark a player as it is for a WD, GD and GK.

3 The first step for young players is to learn how to mark an attacking player, sticking to their opponent like glue to prevent them receiving a pass.

4 When players become more experienced and are more aware of the space on the court, they can then progress to 'defending a space' – preventing an attacking player from moving into a space to receive a pass. Players need to be able to read the game well, anticipating where the next pass will be and moving early to prevent the pass being made.

drill 94 the GK

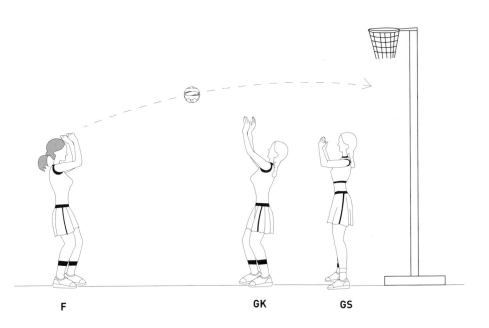

F **GK** **GS**

Objective: For the GK to practise marking the GS, holding a space under the post.

Equipment: One ball and one post between three players.

Description: Start with the GS and GK under the post and a feeder (F) with the ball outside the circle. The GS aims to receive the ball under the post by holding the space, the feeder throwing an overhead pass into the space. The GK marks the GS closely, giving her as little space to move as possible. The GK should try to jump and intercept or 'tip' the ball off court to prevent the GS from receiving the pass, receiving 1 point if she is successful. The GS should shoot if the pass is successful. The drill restarts if the ball is intercepted or a goal is scored.

Coaching points: The GS should face the feeder. The GK should always be between the ball and the GS; if the GS is in front of the GK this allows an easy pass.

Progression: Vary the position of the feeder.

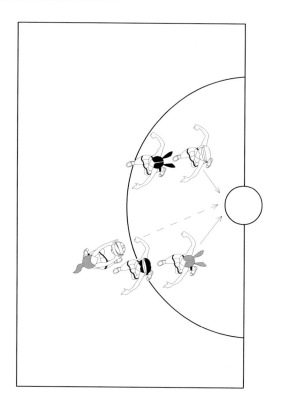

Objective: For GK and GD to practise defending in the circle, and for GS and GA to practise getting free and develop awareness and control of space in the circle.

Equipment: One ball and one post between five players.

Description: GA and GS stand in the circle, defended by the GK and GD. The feeder stands on the edge of the circle. The shooters dodge to get free and indicate where they want to receive the ball. The feeder passes the ball to each shooter in turn. The shooter should then make the shot, following the ball. The second shooter takes control of the space under the post, waiting for the rebound and blocking her defender. The defenders should aim to intercept the ball or get the rebound. Shooters get one point for a goal and two points for a rebound caught. Defenders get one point for an interception and two points for a rebound caught.

Coaching points: Look for close marking from the defenders and confidence in movement, dodging into space and holding space from the shooters.

Progression: Vary the position of the feeder.

half game

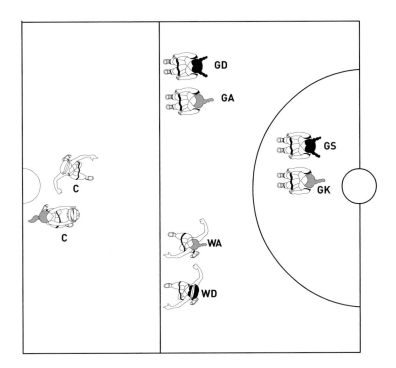

Objective: For players to practise a variety of skills in a game situation.

Equipment: One ball, bibs, half the court between eight players.

Description: Set up a game in half the court to restrict space and allow players to practise specific skills. The coach can apply conditions to the game, for example only chest passes can be used, only WA can receive the centre pass, no passing back to the player from whom you received the ball and so on.

Coaching points: Look for good quality passes and movement towards the ball to receive a pass. A free pass can be given to the opposite team if a condition is not applied. Check players' understanding of the drill regularly. Any loose ball should be chased.

Jane Altschwager (the Swifts, Australia) demonstrates a good shooting action, with the GD defending the shot well.

WARMING DOWN

At the end of the session the players will be hot and probably tired. It is a mistake to just say, 'Thanks for coming' and let them wander off. Instead, you should always incorporate a warm-down to develop good habits and provide a number of important functions:

- a great opportunity to work on flexibility as the muscles are warm
- allows the body to begin to flush out many of the waste products produced during vigorous exercise
- represents a clear end to the session, ensuring that players feel they have had a well thought out, well-structured session, which all adds to the atmosphere of excellence and care that will motive a group to work effectively.

Just as with all the drills, the warm-down sessions must focus on form; only strict form will provide the intended benefits.

drill 97 *hamstring reach*

Objective: To improve flexibility and warm down the body.

Equipment: One ball per player.

Description: Line the players up along the base line with their feet over shoulder width apart and the ball between their feet. On the coach's command, the players reach down (keeping their legs straight at all times), pick up the ball and place it as far back through their legs as they can. The players then walk backwards until their feet are in line with the ball once more, and repeat the drill. The aim is to cover the given distance (approximately 10 m) in as few pick-ups as possible.

Coaching points: Watch for cheats who bend their legs to gain an advantage. This is a slow, controlled drill and form is everything.

Objective: To improve flexibility.

Equipment: One ball per player.

Description: Line the players up with their right side facing into court, their feet over shoulder width apart, their legs straight and the ball in front of their left foot. On the coach's command, the players bend down (keeping their legs straight), pick up the ball and place it in front of their right foot. Leaving the ball where it is, the players then swap feet, progressing into the court, so that the ball is by their left foot once more. The movement is then repeated for a set distance before the players return to the start; 10 m is more than enough for this drill.

Coaching points: Watch for cheats who bend their legs to gain an advantage.

drill 99 circle stretch

Objective: To improve flexibility.

Equipment: One ball between six players.

Description: Players form a circle with their feet over shoulder width apart and touching the feet of the next players. Keeping their legs straight, the players reach down and hang their hands as close to the floor as possible. The ball is rolled from one player to another around the circle. After ten passes in total, walk the players around for a minute and then repeat.

Coaching points: Watch for cheats who bend their legs to gain an advantage.

Progression: If you have enough players, form two or more groups and race to see which is the first to complete the passes.

drill 100 circle stretch 2

Objective: To improve flexibility.

Equipment: One ball between about six players.

Description: The players sit facing outwards in a circle with their feet wide apart and touching the feet of the next players. The ball is passed in order around the circle. Each player must give and take the ball with two hands every time.

Coaching points: This drill provides a stretch to the backs of the legs and requires good flexibility in order to be able to rotate the trunk and make the pass. If players are short on flexibility they will creep their bottoms away from the group so that they are leaning back rather than sitting upright. Encourage them to keep their legs nice and straight throughout.

Progression: If you have enough players, form two or more groups and see which is first to complete the passes. Vary the direction of the pass on command.

Objective: To improve flexibility.

Equipment: Half the court.

Description: Line the players up facing into court. Keeping the body upright, they should take a slow, controlled stride forwards. The stride should be as large as control will allow. Repeat over a set distance (10 m is fine) and then walk the players back to the start and repeat.

Coaching points: This drill only works if the body is strictly upright with a 'proud' chest and the head up. The more slowly this drill is performed, the better. The challenge is for each player to beat her own score; if they can cover the distance in five strides, they should try to cover it in four and a half next time and so on.